Ōoka Makoto, distinguished Japanese poet and critic, believes "there is hope for modern poetry precisely because the age is so complex: because humans possess words, live by means of words, live words, are words themselves. Since words are the basic bond holding together and making possible history and society, poetry . . . finds in crisis the profoundest of all reasons to go beyond itself and live as it has never done before."

This book brings together long selections from and clear introductions to the work of eight major Japanese poets from three living generations. Each voice here has achieved an individual and compelling way of working words into shapes that mirror that bond between individuals and societies, between past and future.

Asian Poetry in Translation: Japan
Editor, Thomas Fitzsimmons

This project is supported by a grant from the National Endowment for the Arts.

A Play of Mirrors

Asian Poetry in Translation: Japan #7

TRANSLATORS AND CRITICS

Akai Toshio
Brenda Barrows
Christopher Drake
William I. Elliot
Christan Flood
Kamura Kazuo
Kinoshita Tetsuo
Koriyama Naoshi
Kagiya Yokinobu
Takako Lento
Edward Lueders
Miura Masashi
Onuma Tadayoshi
Tsuruoka Yoshihisa
Kirsten Vidaeus

Calligraphy by Ōoka Makoto

Book Design and Art by Karen Hargreaves-Fitzsimmons

A Play of Mirrors

Eight Major Poets of Modern Japan

Edited by

ŌOKA MAKOTO

THOMAS FITZSIMMONS

YOSHIOKA MINORU
TAMURA RYŪICHI
IIJIMA KŌICHI
TADA CHIMAKO

ŌOKA MAKOTO
TANIKAWA SHUNTARŌ
SHIRAISHI KAZUKO
YOSHIMASU GŌZŌ

KATYDID BOOKS
Oakland University

Rochester, Michigan

1987

Copyright © 1987 by Akai Toshio, Brenda Barrows, Christopher Drake, William I. Elliot, Thomas Fitzsimmons, Christan Flood, Kagiya Yokinobu, Kamura Kazuo, Kinoshita Tetsuo, Koriyama Naoshi, Edward Lueders, Onuma Tadayoshi, Ōoka Makoto, Kirsten Vidaeus

First Edition

Renga—Linked Poems from *Rocking Mirror Daybreak* by Ōoka Makoto and Thomas Fitzsimmons published with the permission of Chikuma Shobo Publishing Co., Tokyo
English versions of the poems of Tanikawa Shuntarō published with the permission of Prescott Street Press, Portland, Oregon

Produced by K T DID Productions

Printed in the United States of America on acid free paper by Thomson-Shore, Dexter, Michigan
Set in Bembo by Sans Serif Typesetters, Ann Arbor, Michigan

Library of Congress Cataloging in Publication Data

A Play of mirrors.

    (Asian poetry in translation. Japan ; #7)
    1. Japanese poetry—20th century—Translations into English. 2. English poetry—Translations from Japanese. 3. Japanese poetry—History and criticism.
I. Ōoka, Makoto, 1931– . II. Fitzsimmons, Thomas, 1926–
III. Yoshioka, Minoru, 1919– . IV. Series.
PL782.E3P54 1987   895.6'15'08   86-21130
ISBN 0-942668-09-X (alk. paper)
ISBN 0-942668-08-1 (pbk. : alk. paper)

ERRATA
Title Page verso and p. 311: Kamura should be Kawamura; Elliot, Elliott.
P. 239: last line and all of p. 240 should follow p. 241.
P. 246: #8, line 3, "keep" should be "kept";
. . . #8, line 12, "than" should be "then".
Apologies

Contents

The Poems

The Poems

***Renga*—Linked Poems**

TANIKAWA SHUNTARŌ (1931-   )

The Poems

Introduction

Modern Japanese Poetry — Realities and Challenges

By Ōoka Makoto

Written poetry in Japan has a history of more than thirteen centuries. The first great Japanese poet, Kakinomoto Hitomaro, wrote during the last two decades of the seventh century. His poems are included along with those of several hundred other known and anonymous ancient poets in the *Man'yōshū* (*Collection for Myriad Ages*), an anthology containing 4,516 poems in all — poems that are even today widely read and studied. A dozen or so major works — monographs, exegeses, commentaries, essays — on the *Man'yōshū* appear annually and some of them sell exceptionally well.

In how many countries is a poetic form that was perfected more than a thousand years ago not only the object of extremely specialized research but also avidly read by people in all walks of life? This phenomenon reflects an important characteristic of modern Japanese culture as a whole. Modern Japan contains any number of delicate fusions of ancient and modern in its arts, politics, and social dynamics. When, for example, a large electronics firm using state-of-the-art technology constructs a new factory, the ground-breaking ceremony is presided over by a Shinto priest who recites and sings ancient charms and incantations believed to have the power to purify the construction site. This kind of juxtaposition of old and new can be seen in so many aspects of daily life in modern Japan that the Japanese are often not aware of them.

The imperial family itself was originally the highest-ranking priestly clan overseeing state rituals. The imperial court was and continues to be the largest and most carefully kept repository of ancient ritual and incantation, although in considerably polished and edited form. In fact, the history of the Waka, the dominant form of court poetry for centuries, is inseparable from the history of a series of prestigious court anthologies, each edited in the name of the then-reigning emperor. The first of these imperial anthologies was the *Kokinshū* (*Ancient and Modern Collection*), which was completed in about 905. Twenty more followed it in the next five centuries or so. These imperial anthologies—especially the *Kokinshū* and the *Shinkokinshū* (*New Ancient and Modern Collection*), which was completed in 1206—achieved unsurpassed heights of refined beauty that have left a permanent and incalculable influence on subsequent Japanese culture.

The courtly tradition, like all others, eventually lost its vision and vigor. Then in the late 19th century, when Japan began its rapid process of Westernization, the Waka (now usually called Tanka, or "short song") also underwent swift and wrenching changes. It left forever the sphere of courtly values and came to be written by ordinary people, people who used it to express new feelings and perspectives in strikingly new ways. The Tanka form was renovated, not abandoned; crisis resulted in renaissance.

Amazingly, the ancient Tanka form came to be used expressively and subtly by a number of outstanding modern poets. The form continues to grow in popularity, and it is presently used by at least a million Japanese. The brevity of the Tanka makes it very effective as occasional verse—for capturing the fleeting yet permanently moving emotions evoked by the small events of everyday life. This continued life and development of the Tanka is a major reason why modern Japanese readers and poets continue to be passionately drawn to the ancient *Man'yōshū* anthology.

The standard Tanka contains only thirty-one syllables, which fall into five rhythmic units or "lines" of 5, 7, 5, 7 and 7 syllables. One poetic form, however, is even shorter than the Tanka. Originally called Haikai, it is now referred to as haiku. In the Japanese medieval period the first three lines of the Tanka developed into an independent 17-syllable form having three lines of 5, 7, and 5 syllables. Haiku were originally linked together in sequences, but in the late 19th century they, like the Tanka, were the subject of intense Western-stimulated reform and experimentation and soon developed into self-sufficient poems standing by themselves. As a result of this haiku renaissance, the modern haiku form is fully as popular as the modern Tanka. It is appealing above all because of its extreme brevity, which requires suggestion rather than statement. The haiku lover is also a lover of silence.

To give foreign readers some sense of what these two traditional forms are actually like, I would like to quote a Tanka and a haiku by Masaoka Shiki

(1867–1902), a poet who played a major role in the modernization of both. Although Shiki died of pulmonary tuberculosis when he was only thirty-five, his creatively militant theories and the examples of his own poems were the single greatest reforming influence on traditional Japanese poetry. Although Shiki was confined to his bed for the last six years of his life by spinal tuberculosis, his creative power and energy lasted until the very end. In addition to Tanka and haiku, Shiki also kept a journal during his last years which ranks as one of the masterpieces of early modern Japanese prose.

One winter day Shiki heard voices exclaiming that it was snowing outside—a rare sight. Since he was unable to get up and go see the snow, Shiki wrote a haiku instead:

> Again and again
> I ask how deep
> the snow

As in most haiku, the poet's own feeling is not directly expressed. Yet Japanese readers can feel deep within this extremely reticent poem the bedridden poet's desperate, irrepressible curiosity and longing to see the falling snow and can sympathize and feel pity at the snow drifting through Shiki's heart.

Another day, Shiki lay watching the early summer flowers that were blooming in his small garden. Filled with a premonition that his death was not far away, he wrote ten Tanka to the flowers as if to say goodbye to each of them. One of them:

> Iris petals
> begin to open—
> the last spring
> I will ever see
> almost gone

The Tanka form, because it is somewhat more spacious than the haiku, allows the poet to state or develop an emotion: it is essentially lyric. In Shiki's Tanka, the rebirth of a small flower in his garden contrasts poignantly with his own sense of impending death. His love of the flower makes his own life seem all the more precious and all the harder to leave behind. Yet both the Tanka and the haiku value reticence and indirect suggestion to a degree perhaps unequaled in other poetic traditions.

In the vortex of contending theories and styles that overtook late 19th-century Japan, a new poetic form emerged that had no relation to either the Tanka or the haiku: colloquial free verse. A number of outstanding free-verse poets soon began writing about things and themes that could not be expressed in the shorter traditional forms.

When the Tokugawa shogunate, which had ruled Japan for two and a half centuries, was overthrown in 1868, one of the first acts of the new Meiji regime was to reverse the closed-door policy toward other nations that had been in effect since 1635. The new Japanese rulers, alarmed by the expansionist policies of Europe, Russia, and the United States, threw themselves behind a crash program of Westernization in order to keep Japan from becoming another colony of one of the Western powers. Ironically, however, in their effort to "catch up" with the West, Japan's rulers created a European-style absolutist state of their own. Thus the Japan of the late 19th and early 20th centuries was an explosive mixture of rapid imitation of Western models on the one hand and reactionary nationalism— including colonization of surrounding areas of Asia—on the other.

Poetry, of course, was also torn in different directions at once. Yet free verse was able to hold its own. More and more young poets began to write it, and translations of Western poetry grew in quality and quantity. Growing numbers of readers, dissatisfied with the Tanka and the haiku, also began to passionately read and discuss free verse, thus laying the foundation for the next generation of free-verse poets. The free verse written before World War Two, however, is usually distinguished from that written after 1945. Japan's military defeat had very large repercussions in every part of its society and culture, and postwar Japanese poetry differs markedly from its predecessors. Japanese free-verse poetry written between 1945 and around 1960 is often referred to as "postwar" poetry. In relation to the Tanka and the haiku, however, free verse written from 1945 to the present is usually called "modern" poetry.

Free verse, now entering its second century in Japan, was from the beginning influenced in various ways by new Western trends and movements, from romanticism and symbolism in the 19th century to dada and surrealism in the 20th. Japanese literary criticism was also deeply influenced. In fact, it is impossible to describe modern Japanese literary criticism without mentioning its connections with French symbolist theory. In poetry the links were even closer.

Many of the Western influences were not, however, unambiguous. When, as has happened so often in history, the spiritual and intellectual products of a more highly articulated and developed cultural area move across boundaries into a less sophisticated area, changes in form and quality occur, since the less developed area must assimilate the foreign influences within the configurations of its own traditions and perspectives. The poets and scholars of ancient Japan, for example, revered the larger civilization of China and worked strenuously to understand and adopt it, yet they always chose with great care what they imported and how they imported it. Thus the great T'ang-period poets Li Po and Tu Fu were not widely read in Japan because these poets often expressed great anger at political conditions and their own personal situation, condemning and even cursing a whole range of public targets—all subjects frowned on at the Japanese court of the 10th and 11th centuries. It was the milder Po Chü-i who became the most read and loved Chinese poet in Japan. But it was only the nostalgic Po musing on the beauties of nature who became so popular; all of the political poems full of righteous anger and admonition by Po the advisor and Minister of Justice were carefully edited out of Japanese editions. Li Po, Tu Fu, and even Po Chü-i were not fully understood and did not exert a deep influence until the late 17th century, when Matsuo Bashō wrote. Bashō's own life and poetry allowed—and required—him to grasp this neglected side of the Chinese poets.

A somewhat similar situation arose when Japanese poetry collided with Western poetry in the process of Japanese Westernization. This is why 1945 is such a crucial dividing line.

The year 1945 brought many new experiences to the Japanese. It was, first of all, the first experience of defeat for Japan as a nation-state. Second, it was the year the nuclear age began with two unspeakably destructive atomic bombs being exploded over Hiroshima and Nagasaki. Third, it was the year the militarism and fanaticism that had ruled Japan since the early 1930s were militarily crushed and the ultranationalistic ideology that had supported the militarist system was discredited and destroyed. Fourth, it was the year the Allies occupied Japan and instituted American-style democracy, setting off far-reaching changes in the Japanese political, economic, and social systems, symbolized by the establishment of a new national constitution. The reorganization of the Japanese educational system during the American occupation is a striking example of how traditional Japanese society was shaken to its foundations. Fifth, 1945 was the year of burned-out cities, hunger, black markets, homeless children, the wounded, and almost every other kind of hardship—a situation that did not improve until the economy began to recover during the Korean War. Eliot's *The Waste Land* and Auden's *The Age of Anxiety* seemed to many Japanese titles that summed up their own country. And wars of many kinds continued to break out, in China, in Korea, in Algeria, in Hungary, in Cuba, and on and on.

In 1945 I was fourteen. I still remember clearly how, during the years after that, I and many of my anxious generation felt not so much that we were living in the postwar period as that we had now entered the prewar period before World

War Three. Most of the poems I wrote when I was around twenty, even the love poems, also deal with this "prewar" world. In this I was far from being alone.

These, then, were some of the elements haunting Japan's so-called "postwar" poetry. War experiences, hunger, atomic bombs—they and much more engraved themselves in the minds of Japanese poets and made death a central and commonly used image. But by experiencing global war and nuclear destruction Japanese poets also learned to view personal tragedies as tragedies on a world scale, a perspective denied to Japanese poets writing before World War Two. Now Japanese poets were forced, whether they wanted to or not, to look through their individual fates and see the fate of the whole 20th century. Only after World War Two was Japanese poetry ready to absorb concretely the real meaning of European movements such as dada, surrealism, expressionism, Neue Sachlichkeit, and existentialism. Most of these movements arose after World War One and had been known and discussed in Japan during the 1920s and 30s, but it was only after the Japanese experienced nuclear war, rubble, and hunger that the real force of these movements came home to them. It was the same kind of process the poems of Li Po, Tu Fu, and Po Chü-i had had to pass through, only this time the gap was shorter.

And it was only after World War Two that the basic attitudes and concepts expressed in Paul Valery's cultural criticism, T.S. Eliot's *The Waste Land*, André Breton and Philippe Soupault's *Les champs magnétiques*, Breton and Paul Éluard's *L'Immaculée Conception*, and similar works made sense in Japan and evoked a profound, sympathetic response.

Behind this sympathy lay the new conviction that poetry was an alternative to religion and science that could successfully resist the devastation, mass death, and despair surrounding the modern world. No matter how optimistic this belief may seem now, postwar Japanese poetry could not have set out without it, because when the Japanese experienced two atomic bombs they also witnessed, symbolically, a vision of apocalypse utterly without divine presence. This is why the demand "Bring back totality through poetry" was common to every group and trend in postwar Japan until at least the 1960s.

Technically, postwar Japanese poetry became incomparably more conscious of itself, raising sense to the level of thought and embodying thought at the level of sense. Greater attention was paid to metaphor and imagery, but the heightened interest in technique was above all a part of the demand for the restoration of totality through poetry. In addition to having to live with vivid memories of war horrors—experienced on the Asian mainland, the South Pacific, in Japan itself— most poets also had to fight off poverty and hunger on a daily basis. This made all the stronger their desire to find in poetry a kind of spiritual salvation—their desire to make poetry responsible for expressing their dream of totality. Thus the fruitful union of strong social criticism and surreal images in the poems of the major postwar poets. Thus the inseparable union of lyricism and cultural criticism. A poet, in other words, also had to be a penetrating critic. Throughout the history of Japanese poetry, from ancient times until the end of the 19th century, almost every major poet was also a powerful critic. In fact, it was not until around 1920, and for a short time after, that criticism and poetry were regarded as adversaries.

In any case, modern poetry, as an alternative to science and religion, was now required to restore a fundamental unity and totality to human thought and action. This was the great claim made by postwar Japanese poetry.

For poetry, what is the modern age?

For our age, what meaning does poetry have?

Both questions are, of course, very difficult to answer. They are made all the more difficult by the fact that each question intertwines with the other in extremely dark and subtle ways. Yet poets have to ask these questions every moment they are poets. The incredible advances made by modern science and the violent social changes they bring about—changes that affect the smallest corners of our daily life—make the answers even harder to find.

Science, the brilliant weapon for conquering poverty, ignorance, superstition, and suffering; science, which developed as the advance guard for opposing and overcoming absolutism, tyranny, and oppression; this same science now dares to pursue not only nuclear fission and fusion but even genetic engineering and artificial brain-cell expansion. These experiments, of course, can easily turn into destructive attacks on the very basis of human life. The gigantic dual potential and contradictions inherent in science symbolize the central dilemma now faced by humanity as a whole. Yet it is impossible to conceive of a future without science. Neither can the poet ignore it.

In the 1970s science brought to Japan, as elsewhere, new electronic technologies including everything from photocopy and video equipment to vending machines and procedures that make possible the immediate copying and large-scale dissemination and circulation of something which was momentarily known as an "original." Poetry cannot help but be influenced by this historical trend. What is called the "copy civilization" or "copy society" in Japan takes from the hands of the poet poems that were written in a non-reproducible realm of experience and almost instantly spreads them indiscriminately in every direction. Radical thinning and weakening is inevitable. Even the concept of originality, which underlies so many myths about poetry, is in urgent need of reconsideration.

But there is hope for modern poetry precisely because the age is so complex: because humans possess words, live by means of words, live words, are words themselves. Since words are the basic bond holding together and making possible

history and society, poetry—which exists in order to search for the most funda-
mental ways and usages of words—finds in crisis the profoundest of all reasons to
go beyond itself and live as it has never done before.

Yoshioka Minoru

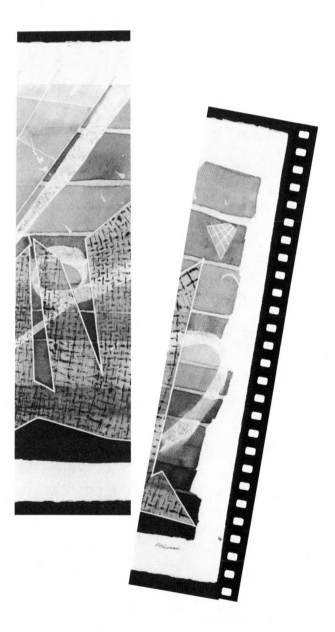

Yoshioka Minoru

by Tsuruoka Yoshihisa

Yoshioka Minoru was born on April 15th, 1919. The years from 1941 to 1945 he spent as a soldier in the Pacific War. The first collection of his poems was compiled and edited in two days when he received the summons to the colors. Entitled *Liquid*, this book came out on December 10th, 1941, and the author received his copies on an arctic battlefield in Manchuria. The only book to come out of Yoshioka's twenties, *Liquid* is in more than one sense a memento of his adolescence.

Yoshioka's early poems were distinctly colored by the Japanese modernist movement (which flourished around such central figures as Kitazono Katsue and Haruyama Yukio) of the latter half of the 1920s. *Liquid* thus features poems at once lyrical and surrealist.

> Pull out from under a tree on a festival day of the Blessed Virgin
> Parenthesize a desert into the brain's afternoon. . .

Every poem in *Liquid* is a series of *non sequiturs* devoid of any "story," and this tendency is carried forward into Yoshioka's later poems which will no doubt resist translation more than any other Japanese poet's. Yoshioka's poems are aggregates of magical images produced by an aesthetic consciousness which is well-nigh esoteric.

In "How I Write Poems?" Yoshioka tells us how his poems come into being.

I start my poems with no premeditated themes or structures. For me a blank sheet of paper is always the best place for poetry. . . . I become calmly saturated with a certain consciousness and a certain composition, and reality is established. Then come moments of white heat. I'm visited with ennui, and then by despair. I see a certain painting. A female body is imagined. I touch a substance hard as a tortoise-shell. A man who has been walking on planks goes away. Next float up the shape of a perambulator and the two Chinese characters for "vegetable". . .

Judging from this, Yoshioka's method is not very far from automatic writing, his pen moving to catch alive spontaneous images stirring in the stream of his consciousness.

Still Life was published in 1955, and *Monk* in 1958. This latter established Yoshioka Minoru as one of the most important Japanese poets today. In it what lies at the unfathomable bottom of everyday life is scooped up and crystallized by means of a poetic language which has enhanced its hardness considerably.

> . . . a royal road the still-born child will open
> into a primeval virgin land
> and there he will see
> the future delivery scene
> the maternal lightning torn open
> & from that immense bloody darkness out will come
> white-haired still-born children one after the other. . .
>
> "Still-Born"

Yoshioka's "war experience" is doubtless what lies behind these lines: his own words refer to them as "the first of its kind among my poems in which I tried, in my own fashion, to get involved with the outside world." But it is not the actualities of that world, such as might have been encountered by the poet during the war, for example, that are approached here. Rather, this world described is an irrational one (somehow reminiscent of nothingness itself) of a "mother" and her "still-born child" who are irrevocably estranged from everything that is alive. Perhaps in Yoshioka's eyes the inhumanity experienced during the war and the "false" peace of the postwar period were judged to be on a par. Here is a tragedy found to be persisting from the "primeval" times and far into the "future." The "white-haired still-born child" born out of "that immense bloody darkness" of "torn" maternity represents the poet's line of vision, if somewhat grotesque, refusing to be reconciled to the actualities of the world. Perhaps *Monk* can be viewed as a concentrated linguistic warfare in which Yoshioka tried to dispose *en masse* of the lyrical modernism and the "war experience" that were within himself. Everywhere in *Monk* we meet bitter humor and almost secret love for man and his world. And we now realize that this love or eroticism is what has enabled Yoshioka to break fresh poetic ground. The enmity long harbored against the world, and perhaps also against the poet's own being, now receding to a vanishing point, Yoshioka's poetry obtains a rhythm quite relieved and free together with a certain velocity.

In *Quiet House* (pub. 1968) the above tendency is still more apparent.

> I always think of that
> Soft horror of a door knob
> What is a stay?
> Look at a huge musical instrument popping open at a scene of a fire
> Ridicule I shall not
> What is not to be seen
> A woman's waist in my arms I go sliding
> The circle that circles shun
> There is a sausage coming back along its circuit
> After dividing up all realities
> It is a new conception. . .
>
> "Stay"

The "soft horror of a door knob" speaks very well the characteristic feature of this volume. Formerly, Yoshioka's horror was stiff and stood upright in the dark, much like a knife of ice. Here, however, horror has turned into a soft knob, just like the limp clock of a Salvador Dali. Bright streams of light shine into these poems now, as if our poet is allowed to "stay" in the world that he has long been repulsing. Perhaps a certain "postwar surgery" has been successfully concluded in Yoshioka Minoru. Another thing that merits mention here is Yoshioka's marriage (his earnest love for his wife Yōko is well-known) which coincided with the writing of the poems included in the present volume. There have been numerous cases, Éluard's for one, where the presence of a female played a vital role in calling poetry into being. "A woman's waist in my arms I go sliding/The circle that circles shun. . ."—these lines seem to exude a very healthy kind of eroticism. We also find a sort of solidarity consciousness quickening in *Quiet House*, and this is in such a striking contrast to the sense of desolation which marked *Monk*. Here is how "Stay" ends:

I think of that
Tiny love under the umbrella
The driving wheel of a speeding car
Veering more and more sharply to the left. . .

This fresh "love" and this velocity: from here Yoshioka's poetry inaugurates its new development.

Saffron Gathering (pub. 1976) won the Takami Jun Prize (which is annually awarded to the best collection of poems of the year), and this occupies by far the most important place in the whole of Yoshioka Minoru's poetical achievements.

. . . And yet you are wet
As rain itself
The blood on the wings of that dove
Gone to hide in a field of leeks
Form and yet no form
The crime of pure happiness which needs only to be unveiled
Cut the inner facet of the marble
Iris/   stripes incarnadine/   autumn/   Alice
Liddel!

"My Approaches to Alice"

Departing from the imagery-oriented and high-velocity poems of the late 1960s and returning once more to the dry, hard language of his earlier poems (and thereby recovering sense, if only to a limited extent), Yoshioka now offers a still new type of poetry to the reader. Evidently, the experiment with language which he has been pursuing has reached maturity, and the result is the ever involved syntax woven into complex layers of images resembling diamond needles, and the eroticism which can be surprisingly realistic from time to time. Yoshioka has completely surmounted the futile influence of the Japanese modernist movement of the prewar period. He now elegantly stands on a totally new poetic ground that is his alone.

Yoshioka's poetry owes much to the act of seeing. His eyes, sharp as a bird's and forever shining with curiosity, take nourishment from a wide variety of things—paintings, dances, plays, the swinging breasts of a stripteaser, and so on.

Also, as is increasingly noticeable in *Saffron Gathering* and *Summer Banquet* (pub. 1979), Yoshioka now willingly admits the words of other poets, writers and painters into his own poems. "If only her petals curled up a little more" says one of the opening lines of "My Approaches to Alice", and this quotation from Lewis Carroll proves a happy one, like many others. The adept use of citations in Yoshioka now makes for a very enjoyable kind of poetry, much like Ezra Pound's.

30

In his own words, Yoshioka has introduced into Japanese poetry "a celebration in darkness which is at once weird and refined, scatological and lofty, comical and serious."

Yoshioka Minoru has many friends, mostly poets and painters, who were born in the 1930s, but relatively few of his own age. Perhaps it is the distinct youthfulness of his poetry that enables this poet to enjoy such a tremendous influence on poets who are still in their twenties. Also a talented book-designer and a very warm person, this elegant poet of stature occupies a place that is unique among the poets now writing in Japanese.

Yoshioka Minoru
The Poems

Tenderhearted Firebug

Charlie always wishes he did not have to
trim a bald head in the middle of summer
much less shave a little girl's face
fuzz all around her mouth
so indecent it makes you think of the rainy season
like the belly of a milk-drinking doll
Charlie the barber would like to paw the white scalp
of a refrigerator every day
it's got guts almost ready to go off
like the fine fire engine bell Charlie loves
fish for cats lined up dead
coke bottles tinkling
Charlie wants his water ice cold
& his formless tears frozen
no memory of ever being a little boy
but a record of setting forest fires 14 times
32 year old Charlie
is a screaming photograph of war that will never fade
flying his mother & sister like gulls
over blood
is also a pulley chuting down through a total blackout
if a beard makes the grownup
then Charlie is a grownup pickled in vinegar
the poisonless sardine meat in the barracuda's mouth
if obesity is a sin

then Charlie's body weight is zero
his head is the tail of an American mouse on fire
a ring of fire
spinning round & round
it's something more metaphysical than electricity
Charlie's imprecating heart like a skinned rabbit
juts out from other people's thick-coated humanity
it's a painting in paroxysm
not an infection in cold contempt
of the general public but a general infection
the red of yellow wax closed
to other people's prying
Charlie's escape drama
see Charlie in flight
from one iron pole to another
from the American upper air stream
to the india ink China sea of torn sharks?
other people's hearts are not hot enough to ignite a match
but even today even this afternoon
tenderhearted firebug Charlie Colden
drools hot saliva
real forests are all lonely beds that produce fire
cigarette filter celluloid box
Charlie's tools are all very small
they transform everybody's mundane ordinariness
into an extraordinary octave
junk art
is this a victory of Charlie's anti-commercialism
from other people's balcony in South Canyon
a comforting pillar of flames can be seen in the distance at night
Charlie refuses to run away
he will on the contrary visit
or on the contrary he will stand still

the weak eyes of a cicada perched on a rock
forbid seeing
the black branched joys of living
the beautiful way of death
practiced by milkmaids & birds
the bridal dress beyond the trailing smoke
a fire in his head Charlie is
putting out the burning wings   the fire of self
"the rain gear   don't forget your rain gear"
        "the rain gear   don't forget your rain gear"
tenderhearted Charlie Colden
discharges into a tortoise shell
till the rainy season nears

Sentimentality

I

pull down the steel shutters
no commonplace habits mine
even my mind is steel-clad
I'm a man hiding in a box
seen & remembered by a plumber who just happens to be passing by
the girl who laughs at me
as I squat in the toilet
is eating a peach with her back turned
she hates the hammer of the plumber who has his hat pulled well over his eyes
because he would not let her use the water to wash her peach
& caused the narrow source of honey to run dry
the girl who is still in her young-bag days
still ignorant of a grownup woman's summer of sweat
will someday come running too
into my box house
will hug the deformed pillar at the entrance to the law office out front
until then temporarily closed
let a giraffe run all the way down from the roof to the bed
& paint the whole place
already it's as dark in here as a cathedral

II

a lotus opens on the water in a goldfish bowl
the beginning of a bad season
the girl is changing beneath thin skin
begins to transfer black juice from the crown of a flowering plant
into an opaque lobster-shaped bag
it is then that birds fly through the rain-wet bush in my nostrils
all the narrow necked bottles
on the shelf in the darkness
begin to itch & quiver
what change am I waiting for
what exchange

III

the sliced surface of my sleep becomes smooth as agate
the one woman who happened to be there
a handsome-limbed woman in deceptive widow's weeds has been with me since
    yesterday
underneath my magnanimous carnal desire now
as a composition of leg lines
the upper half of her body has been at my service since morning
especially the nebula of pretty freckles behind the shoulders
terribly captivates my mind
at moments enlightens
I presume she has committed a murder
if not her sickly husband
then the gallant who can easily shoulder a bag full of potatoes

if not a man then something else
a big-headed salamander perhaps must have been the victim

IV

experience leads me to betray the accused
it is in the nature of the accused that the accused can't be saved
they all make statements well worthy of punishment
for example I'm brought into a court of justice that is merely props
& am surrounded as accused by people in black
     "my wife is that which is sold to the ant world
     & melts   a shining naked bag of sugar" I blurt out
I make an unfavorable impression
& go to jail my shoulders those of a criminal
my lawyer hurries back to his wife kids & parents
his buttocks full of grains his neck the fatted neck of a chicken he goes out
        into the rain
the unfortunate are fed wire & inhabit a dark place

V

the woman's husband is an expert seaport engineer
every day he goes to the sea with a welder
from working long months & years under the sea
the welder when daylight hits him walks crab-fashion
all the hairs on his body shine
bubbles all over the place
bubbles bitter & very sticky
the husband just builds a fire on the shore
a woman pops up
from between a wrecked ship & a broken net
that is to say the engineer's wife brings food & takes a swim
the floor of hot sand changes the human mind into a complicated conch
& sets cold fish jumping about at the same time

the three people's meal after that is dangerous
dishes & forks move dismally
meat & eggs are all consumed without a trace
vegetables are bashfully left over
the sea is filled with dead men

VI

I look again into the lotus flower
no conversion there
none of the cords around the women of the world is undone
frogs too are squeezed tight
I dream of blond hair blown out from the deepest recesses of the flower
I reach my hand to the woman's thigh
in order to save myself & the unfortunate woman
mourning dresses are of a color & a shape very difficult to distinguish from
    night
besides they slip off when the time comes
after that I am a faithful game keeper
make up my mind to raise the chicks found in the grass
I hear the woman's voice now changed to that of a water-hen wading near the
    shore
in a shack safely away from all laws & smog
well protected from all vulgar foods
I lay siege to a beautiful castle of teeth all alone
& win all the other beautiful spoils
the setting sun is that which shines
& sobs
a waterfall hangs from the woman's hair & freezes
calmly I read the golden syntax of the Code
let's see now I think I have served the woman pretty well
let the sinful woman go then
long shall I wait now for the peach-girl to arrive with a child who looks like
        the plumber & press me for marriage

Monks

I

four monks
lounge about in the garden
sometimes they assume the shape
of sticks on which black cloth is rolled
without hatred
they flog a young woman
until bats shriek
one prepares the meal
another goes out in search of sinners
a third abuses himself
a fourth gets himself killed by a woman

II

four monks
each devoting himself to service
bringing down the holy figurine
hoisting a cow onto the cross
one shaves the head of another
the dead one prays
still another makes a coffin
just then a flood of childbirths come surging in from the midnight village
in unison the four of them get to their feet
four disabled umbrellas

beautiful walls & linings on the ceiling
a hole appears there
& rain begins to fall

III

four monks
come to the table for supper
the one with long arms deals out the forks
the one with warts pours out wine
the other two don't show their hands
but touching today's cat
& future's woman
their hands mold a thickly haired image
in which are embodied both woman and cat
flesh is that which fastens bones
flesh is that which is washed in blood
two of them grow fat from eating
the other two lose flesh from making

IV

four monks
go out for morning penance
one in the shape of a bird goes to the wood to welcome a hunter
another in the shape of a fish to the river to peep at the maid-servants' crotches
a third comes back from town as a horse carrying a load of weapons
a fourth sounds the bell because he is dead
never do the four burst out laughing in unison

V

four monks
plant seeds in the fields

by mistake one of them dedicates
a turnip to the buttocks of a child
the mouth of its astonished mother whose face is ceramic
sinks a sun of red mud
three of the monks are singing in chorus
on a very high trapeze
the dead one
tries his voice inside the throat of a nesting crow

VI

four monks
lean over a well
goats' scrotums to wash
too many menstruation belts to wash
three of them join efforts to wring
a sheet the size of a balloon
the dead one carries it on his shoulder
& dries it on the tower in the rain

VII

four monks
one of them writes the origin of the temple & the histories of the four
another writes the lives of the world's flower queens
a third writes the histories of the axe & the chariot & the monkey
a fourth because he is dead
hides himself from the others & burns one after another
the histories that the other three write

VIII

four monks
one causes the births of a thousand love children in the land of withered trees

a second lets a thousand love children die in a sea devoid of salt & the moon
a third is surprised to find that a thousand pairs of dead feet & a thousand
        pairs of live eyes weigh exactly the same
on the scale where a snake & grapes are entwined
a fourth though dead is still ill
coughing on the other side of the walls

IX

four monks
abandon the fortress of breastplates
with no life-long fruit of labor to gather
they hang themselves & sneer together
on a place one step higher than the world
and so
the bones of the four retain the thickness of the winter trees
& stay dead till the age comes that will break the ropes

Saffron Gathering

on a palace wall somewhere in Crete
there is said to be a magnificent fresco
"The Gathering of Saffron"
there   a boy on all fours
gathers saffron
among the rocks the sapphire waves repeating convoluted patterns day after day
but were sun to shine on the boy's forehead
though we only see him from behind
salt shaped like stars would surface
when on a promontory in evening the boy's cleft buttocks
thrust out we
recognize the trickle of fragrant sap from a stalk of saffron
waves come   white chopped waves
next the decapitated
beautiful neck of a monkey is displayed
atop the quartz-like cavernously dark
face of the boy whose eyes are shut
like an Arcinboldo portrait
composed of spring fruit & fish
everything putrefies
from the surface
the torso of the monkey
tanned by the faith & curses beneath the Aegean
in the night that even virgin skin cannot resist
the dead blue hair that quivers

what do the boy's shoulders support
is it his nurse's thighs
is it the concealed phallus of the monkey
in the mirror it is reflected
like a hieroglyph
the evening glow of sun colors the distant columns first
waves vanish
going round & round inside a brown conch
"Song" is born
pale purple of saffron flowers
were somebody to beckon to him
the boy will run down the ledge
& choose of all forms of temporary death to drown
as for us   for the time being we   will not tell
should not tell
that old wives' tale about a swimming monkey
until the day when the waves wash over the dome of heaven

Still-Born

I

on a large bib lies a still-born child
nobody's enemy
friend to none
a ghost to perpetuate the lineage of the eternally young
or if humanity exists a crown of thorns on humanity's cursed memory
the stench of the eternal mind cum flesh
the fruit of a handsome soul's sweat
once graven in the mother's mirror & womb
a new arrangement of teeth within the earth's gyre
to be dispossessed by none
at work with the father & straddled in straw
solid buttocks inside honest gravity
but from this day on
no apple of the father's false eye
nor the mother's tiger fondling
no brother to little ones the still-born child
a new personage
in the temple of bunched bacteria
for whom the bell of this freezing century has tolled
sheer terror's tribute
judge judged & onlooker
the film of magnificent identity gyrates
not in the coffin in flames

is the still-born child
nor under the stars of burial clay
but on that side from which it can watch us

II

in another country of nothing but withered trees
the mother washes the body of her still-born child
from a cruel medieval king comes the order
build a palace from all the bones
this servitude of fire done
still-born children go
in flocks & packed inside horses' hooves
away from the land that was raised with the mothers' tears
midday is the torture time favored by the king's men
one mother given to each withered tree
more withered trees & more mothers to hang
a million withered trees sway & a million mothers are torn
a cliff of wombs hangs from an August sky
with fierce eyes the world's mothers see
                              a forest fire

                    hear at the same time
          the cataclysm come to quench the fire

III

the still-born child discovers by chance
that all the beds in the world creak
each politely bearing one old person
out of numberless loose faucets belly worms come
abandoning the old & death
they head in the direction
where busy stomachs are divined
all packed with meat & vegetables
guns are picked up & aimed here & there

shrieks are heard
wishing cleansed happiness to the old
take the blood slowly to the mountain top
& splash it from there on the beds
of those lovers so firmly married to convention
the only thing the still-born child deplores
is that he is not possessed of sex
he is motified as a belly worm
no early morning fornication for him
no soft bed of silk for the still-born child
no cool intimate place in the shade of the wheat field
but the darkness of the mother's mourning dress
to repeat his solitary orgy in
his passionate buddings of stone
forbidden procreation   castrated glory
then learn if possible the science of extinction
it is the season of forest trodden under green satin slippers
the fountain of castration glitters
pumpkins bloom fully
the still-born child shares his bed with all the dead old men of the world

IV

as to the development of the still-born child & his illness
all the doctors keep silent
the rampage of a beast that causes the source of honey & sponge to run dry
no mother's breasts to be seen on any horizon
all cloaked under bad weather & violence
prying can only find
sulfuric acid crystalized
thus the times go astray among the rocks of sorcery
the arithmetic of foxy merchants who send too much autumn fruit
down the river brings about illness

nails don't grow outward on still-born children
but inward to where dreams are conceived
the still-born child's disease
gets worse & worse in direct proportion to
food & the father's timidity
& finally disappears in a dense fog of powder smoke
the still-born child is remembered in no clinical records
but by cemetery violets feeding on historians

V

dead child on her back a mother goes on pilgrimage
in the capital of a world of wax

  a general of moles torn to pieces
  a night camp in the coils of headless horses' intestines
  a violated girl burned roofs visible between her thin thighs
  fish marrying a soldier killed in a marsh in the morning
  men-of-war in spiderweb turrets all sinking
  under the sea chiseled out by the teeth & nails of a coal stoker

a still-born child's favorite spectacles all
but the mother's love is quick
take the tragic toys away from the dead child
train him properly
punish him when disobedient
expose his private parts before ladies & gentlemen at table in broad daylight
from the height where the coats of arms of all the nations in favor of
  night-operations are ripped to pieces
hang the dead child's hair
flourish his hairless slippery head
put him to shame
throw light on the physical humiliations of the father & his brethren
& on the melancholy roses of those men's souls

until pain makes the dead child incontinent
the yellow dead child of a broom
the dead child of marble
the black dead child of iron wire
the dead child of a blond forest the numerous dead children of sand
meanwhile
in a land where trees shelter summer cicadas
a wise mother her voice still tearful but different
makes by means of a different kind of energy
an identical history of anger

VI

the favorite pastime of still-born children
is to team up
& throw a net into the coral sea
cause the heavy testicles of the men who sank with canons to resonate
decorate colorfully women's anuses sucking in sand & darkness
relish perfect peace of mind when working for the dead
break the shackles of salt & iron
patch up the bodies with strong glue
make them serviceable again this time in the land of withered trees
golden fish scales jingle silver fish scales ring
enraptured days with sharks' teeth biting
peaceful bones find the bed service of sea water boring
still-born children can hear them say that
then let's spread the net again from the moon as wide as possible
collect anything that is dead
the mother makes grimaces & won't give a hand
she shouts in her house a wrecked ship
you can't exchange dead things for nothing
the still-born child's voice is too small to insist
he hides himself from the mother's eyes
& lies down on his side quite frozen

& by his side lies the sea
the sea where legend can be traced

VII

when the mother has gone to sleep
the still-born child crawls about on the floor
in the end more still-born children will rise
& fill the sea under a spring storm
faces all upturned as befits the dead
they go jumping about one after another
in search of their violated sister
not just one sister but sisters without number
beckoned by the spirit of the waves
holding funereal flowers over their heads
they go to the sea where blood is mixed & dishonored
& cleanse the pillars of thighs
sisters conceive & sisters bear
innumerable still-born children for a midnight celebration
a royal road the still-born child will open
into a primeval virgin land
& there he will see
the future delivery scene
the maternal lightning torn open
& from that immense bloody darkness out will come
white-haired still-born children one after the other

VIII

mothers arrive each with a dead child
from a certain hemisphere a certain deserted capital
in liveries of mourning dresses all draggle-tailed
a few even with a dog of penitence
they go into the desert until it is filled to capacity
other chattering mothers now forced into silence

move from the village to the seashore
the religious flow of black sashes without a break
lest the dead children should come alive again
humor them with nursery songs & nightmares
& establish dominion throughout this mundane world
how could flesh & blood sing the death of this civilization
together in thunderous chorus
last of all half the widowed mothers line the glacier
see those voluptuous hips
each slapping her child on the buttocks
as proof of possessing a dead child each
& just as the child cries out in pain
this long & difficult night journey of vengeance will end
above the world of mourning dresses
the tip of a pyramid is seen
only when gathered thus without number
will the mothers be able to start a new sky
inside their furious hair
& a constellation of real numbers be laid

Family Photograph

mother wears a traditional underskirt
along the *tamo* tree the hanging tree
the sun rises
in the graveyard of the island
a fierce man eats a hundred thrushes
such is the dark mind of a father full of obligation
o no not again
big sister
still hides the rugby ball
that came rolling from the park
& so the cat who is our lodger
soaked in the rain that runs on the surface of the marsh
like a goblin
little sister is
on a goodwill trip night after star-shiny night
is everybody there now
then we'll take our picture
give us a big smile
face up to the sky
but will we have a good picture I wonder
already I am
in the back country near the Mediterranean
growing up with a cork tree

In Praise of the Old and Senile

an old man   a cheerless naked child and a pelican
                              trailing along after him
establishes
                  against the day when he will die
                        king
                        of the afflicted
the moral character of flesh/the insularity of mind
saws a whole wood and builds   ever so slowly
            a phantom ship
            underneath his night clothes
                        nothing
                        but broken teeth
                        on board
sails forth from his native land farewell
            to piles and lung troubles
rides the deep waves of his skin
turns his hairy wife over wrong side up
            wits are scattered
            jelly fish not seen through
            in the pitch dark
            poison from her breasts
the old man laughs
and laughs   hurrah   banzai   death
            a new experience
                        at least this once

come night cross the frontier it's off the hinges
   rupture proof fish's belly sheds light
   without a break shrinks without a break builds up a terrible
   pressure is erotic won't let the old
   man of decorum go
   to sleep
the old man recollects
         so bewitching
         the moon
         of antiseptic gauze
rather he creates
   all for his own stomach and bladder naturally
hyena howling vulture shrieking desert nights
& cities of stars and equally of sands
& he sits in the middle of a flame inside a shack
   unable
   to excite
   the extravagant blood
   vesseled in a king's heart
      useless
   like a bamboo basket
        left on its face and useless
his is an uneasy world of hair
       no gorgeous naked dancer there
a barber's razor flashes & shaves his big pate
      that cold plaster touch
then moved
the old man
   dead now and therefore beautiful
   a tutelary god
       of kids and pelicans
moved to where he is in nobody's way

Legend

a chair   jumping down from the chair   a cat   close shot of its feet naked in its hair   for a fraction of a second   then gone   sucked into the deep folds of a flower   everybody is surprised nothing like this before   four legs of wood   limp across the floor for a second   come to a sudden   halt in a corner of the room   the chair becomes legend   a man   he knows nothing about the incident   comes out from under the blanket   sets himself in the chair   letting out circulating heat & stench   assiduously he pulls out the tube in his anus   starts to grow in bulk   uncontainable rubber   occupies the whole room   writhes   everything pulsates   pleasure expands contracts   nighttime now   the man's face the cat's face   side by side in the coil of the tube   a long time   darkness grows   the man suppresses his breathing   on the point of extinction he cries   Fire

Tamura Ryūichi

Tamura Ryūichi

by Christopher Drake

Tamura Ryūichi grew up amid destruction, and is one of its most relentless interrogators. His life parallels almost exactly one of the most deadly periods in Japanese history, and his poems continue to uncover deeper levels of damage as they probe the invisible fault lines that cross and recross contemporary Japanese culture.

Tamura's birth on March 18th, 1923, in the Tokyo suburb of Ōtsuka, preceded by less than six months the great Kantō earthquake that devastated the Tokyo-Yokohama area and brought much of the Japanese economy to a standstill. The damage caused by the earthquake and the massacre of six thousand Korean migrant workers and labor organizers that followed immediately after marked, in many ways, the beginning of military-led economic recovery and expansionism that brought war with China (when Tamura was eight) and then war with the U.S. and Britain (when he was nineteen).

As a child Tamura was, of course, aware of these larger events only indirectly. The earthquake, ironically, spared Ōtsuka, and the town quickly became a gathering place for refugees, including many from Tokyo's traditional entertainment and brothel districts. Tamura grew up in a back room of a restaurant run by his mother (his father had been adopted into the family), who had become suddenly prosperous catering to this new population. More than five hundred geishas and hundreds of other entertainers worked in Ōtsuka then, and in the restaurant Tamura watched many of them playing shamisen and dancing night after night. Much of his education was left to his maternal grandparents, who remembered the songs and tales of premodern Tokyo (Edo) and spoke in rhythms from an older, more humorous, and more sensual age that had almost been forgotten during Japan's forced march toward westernization after 1868.

Living in a world largely peopled and run by professional women, and surrounded by these women as they appeared in their off hours and without makeup, Tamura has never been tempted by the romantic adoration of women found in much early modern Japanese poetry. In the 1930s many of the cooks and waitresses and geishas began to come from starving farm families in the north, and they spoke in rough earthy accents; they appeared to Tamura as anything but beautiful innocents. Although Tamura has written some of the most erotic postwar Japanese poems his images avoid a purely esthetic definition of women. Tamura has from the beginning regarded erotic energy as the source rather than the subject of poetry.

Tamura first encountered written poetry while he was a student at a commercial high school in rebuilt downtown Tokyo. "Getting away from Ōtsuka," he recalls, "was a real liberation, an escape from all the falseness of a town trying to keep alive an artificial culture it got secondhand from old Edo. Ōtsuka was like one of those American towns on the Mississippi that pretend to be living in the 19th century and end up living nowhere."[1] At school he hated business classes but liked English poetry, and he spent most of his time writing self-consciously modernist poems with a circle of friends. Tamura claims, however, that his main motive for writing then was to "break away from the conservatism and anachronism of Ōtsuka."[2] He felt an absolute, burning gulf between the night values of the "gay quarters" in which he lived and the "modern" world outside, a world dominated by male writers, militarists, and seemingly endless expanses of noon light.

Tamura's writing and his interest in the poems of Eliot, Auden, Spender, and Day Lewis brought him in contact with a group of poets and translators gathering around poet-critic Ayukawa Nobuo, who in 1939 put out the first issue of *Wasteland*, a magazine of poetry and cultural criticism that took its title but not its spirit from Eliot's poem. Meanwhile, Japan was moving closer to war with the U.S. and Britain, and the magazine was suppressed. The friends scattered, some forever. In 1983 Tamura estimated that ninety percent of his prewar friends were no longer alive.[3]

To escape the draft, Tamura entered Meiji University, where he spent most of his time reading Thomas Mann and Kabuki plays and memorizing traditional Japanese Rakugo comic stories. But student deferment ended in 1943, and Tamura, pockets stuffed with the works of Stendhal, Rimbaud, and the Japanese poet-fictionalist Nagai Kafū, was soon in the navy. He spent the next two years at bases around Japan watching his friends being sent off to kill themselves, many as kamikaze pilots. Luckily he himself was too tall to fit easily into the tiny cockpit of a Zero fighter. He was stationed instead on artillery duty on the Japan Sea coast just north of Kyoto, where an invasion was expected. The invasion never came, and on August 15th, 1945 — the day of the surrender — Tamura was amazed to find himself still alive.

A whole generation of Japanese writers had been sent off to combat and forced to look at more than literature. Many of the survivors wrote vividly of their brutalizing experiences, and many more were unable to put their worlds back together again. When Tamura and his friends regathered in the ruins of Tokyo, however, they were looking instead toward the future, searching for intense fragments of meaning that would make more apparent the deeper deceptions and counterfeit images underlying and making possible modern Japanese culture and society. Tokyo had been reduced to ashes, but bombers had been helpless to touch the invisible wreckage still filling the Japanese sky.

The poets revived *Wasteland* with their poems and essays. It ran for six issues, from September 1947 to June 1948. Then they published *Wasteland Poems 1951*, one of the most influential collections of postwar Japanese writing (it continues to be reprinted). Similar yearly anthologies followed until 1958, and three special collections also appeared. As early as 1953, however, the self-styled intellectual commune began to realize that its seriousness was beginning to give way to pompousness, and the poets started striking out on their own. Tamura's first book of poetry, *Four Thousand Days and Nights*, was published in 1956.

Tamura is the most and least typical Wasteland poet. Like the others, he tried to go beyond prewar modernism, which had imported only the abstract and esthetic aspects of dada and surrealism and ignored their critical edge (several leading surrealist and so-called proletarian poets ended up writing nationalistic poems during the war). Also like the others, Tamura worked toward a critique of world culture through the discovery of universal images. "We weren't just being nihilistic," he says. "We were glad to be the living dead with nothing to lose. We wanted to question the basic principles behind an industrial society based on the illusion of the isolated individual and the deification of economic growth based on war and imperialism. I tried to make my poems into holes or windows that would let me see through the indefinable spiritual waste as well as the obvious spiritual destruction."[4] After 1945, when most people thought the war had ended, Tamura discovered ways to transcend the old anti-philosophical lyric mode and wrote public poetry about the continuing war between the myth of Japanese progress and democratization and the tiny, almost inaudible voices of those who actually looked and listened.

Tamura has been almost uniquely successful, however, in creating fictional speakers in his poems and in breaking away from the confessional monolog voice that obsessed so many prewar — and postwar — poets and novelists. In fact, Tamura considers the greatest work of prewar Japanese literature to be the diary of Nagai Kafū, because Kafū's written "I" is wryly distanced from his self-conscious confessional ego and is thereby enabled to speak something approaching the truth.

Tamura's poems depend for much of their power, paradoxically, on an intuitive grasp of folk rhythms and strategies of self-parody and on the traditional Japanese identification of death with rebirth and sensuality. "Dialog on an Intersection and a Missing Line" is a good example of Tamura's unconscious, almost uncanny use of the Japanese folksong tradition of statement and counterstatement. The choruses of conflicting voices that reverberate at various levels through almost all of Tamura's poems present not only the moanings of modern people trapped in mass society but also echo ancient Japanese elegiac songs and mythic texts in their almost visionary intensity. And not only people. To Tamura the colors of hawks and other birds are colors of the soul.

In *World Without Words* (1962), *Green Thought* (1967), and subsequent works, Tamura moves first to Hōya, on the edge of Tokyo, and then out into the world of insects and animals and even geology, trying to find an alternative to the human-centered universe of industrial civilization without at the same time turning back to feudal irrationalism. He also moves further out of himself and discovers that "I am a grenade thrower/and I am the enemy/. . .I am a bird/ and I am its blind hunter." The visions and countervisions Tamura had while living for more than two years in a wild area near Mount Asama, a live volcano, did not lead to the comforts of the lyric tradition—the reverse side of the isolated self—but toward decomposition and breakdown, forces Tamura seems to hope will decompose the detached, almost Gothic subject of the Western technological tradition: the ultimate ego, he suggests in "Green Conceptual Body," is the hydrogen bomb. There are, however, glimpses in "Green Thought" and other poems of a way of writing and being that does not require a single voice to speak or shout from any specific location. A "global person" laughs from the top of the stratosphere as Tamura tries to identify himself with first this and then that fragment of an always flowing, always streaming "human house."

Recently, in *Happy Century's End* (1983), Tamura begins to close in on a more intimate way of opening up the self. In "My Imperialism" he reasserts the primacy of public poetry in spite of the increasingly subjective demands made by his aging body and in spite of the fact that most of the other Wasteland members have subsided into private sentiment. Nakagiri Masao, for example, is no longer able to say strange, unthinkable things. And when Kuroda Saburō, who spent the last years of his life as chairman of the leftwing Poet's Congress, was buried, his family chose as his epitaph the title of his most purely personal book of poems.

Finally, in "The Other World," Tamura seems to be making a reconciliation with his own near dead. Like his "man with a green face," Tamura breaks company with male poets who link arms and gaze only out to sea, away from Japan and toward ideal beauty.

[1]Conversation with the author, June 5th, 1983.
[2]"10 kara kazoete," *Tamura Ryūichi shishū*, Shichōsha, 1968, p. 88.
[3]Same conversation.
[4]Same conversation.

Tamura Ryūichi

The Poems

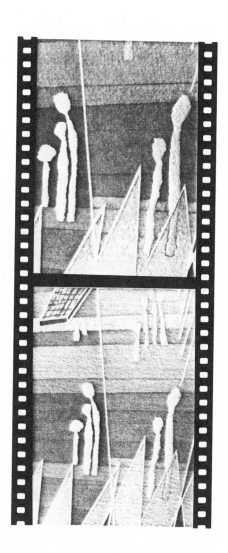

September First

Things that wriggle on the ground
things that walk the earth
I, too, stacked in a living shape
left behind by a casual unsteadiness
in March 1923
six months later, 11:58 a.m., September first
the earth went berserk
convicted our toy-sized modern world
and broke it piece by piece
they say my mother huddled with me
in a clump of clattering bamboos
beyond her arms, in 1939
September first struck the northern hemisphere again
Nazi Germany
directly beneath Poland

And a British-born poet wrote
in a bar on Fifty-Second Street
"We must love one another or die."
thirty years later I walk past
the same bar and pretend it's nothing
did we actually love one another?
yet if we hadn't learned at least the love
of crawling things we would be dead already
crushed by the last light of summer
the earth would be heaving
without us

Green Thought

It is not
blood's rhythm, not
the heart-freezing beat of a poem

Whorl, whirl
too fluid for shape
fundamentally evil

Blinding slopes of light from a global sunset
falling from beyond the stratosphere
soul's gravity

Someone throws open a window
leans halfway out, screams something
screams but it can't be heard

Or
people may have heard the voice
but no one turns around

Or
someone may have turned around
but few people have badly inflamed ears

In this world
sickness is a great privilege
the privilege of things that rot, disintegrate, disappear

This world?
do you mean the world
of oceans, cities, deserts?

Or the world of flesh, concepts, sperm?
have you ever seen a human?
caressed one?

Feverish decaying matter
standing on two legs
giddy with sky in its pores

Whisper the word "love"
humans decompose at once
scream the word "justice"

They disappear instantly,
turn straight to steam, to air—the smallest part
of a heart that pities is enough, so

So don't tiptoe
when you walk on top of graves
nightmares won't jump you

The universe, flames and ashes
burning parts and burnt-out parts
relationships between parts

In parts there is no totality
gather them all, they are not all
parts and parts are another part

I thought time moved in a straight line—
time moves to the measures of parts
differently in different parts

Everything curves
pear tree limb

snake's tongue

Nothing sleeps horizontally
dreams bend around spherical beds
death streams through spherical canals

The conceiving womb curves
the fetus curves
time curves

Spheres closed within spheres
endlessly growing, endlessly dying
green spheres

Float without floating
humans walk without walking
fall without falling

In parts it seems so
in parts we feel it so
in parts we know it so

Close your eyes and understand:
to see with eyes is to massacre
to lay waste

Just once
with eyes not human
to see, to experience

Without time's blind sculpting
to see things
to see the sky

Without driving an emotion
through a wounded dove
through a snake's crushed head

Without aiming emotions at the dead of our time
be of feather, of soft dove breast
be of snake glide over summer grass

Be a gesture of earth that will reenter earth—
if a human child, standing up by itself for the first time
steps, naked, across a doorway

Soaring through its eyes, soaring
from a rainbow-gashed shore toward dark green space
things learning light

If humans have eyes
eyes they hope to see with
they must not look around

Even if a spherical human
shouts from a spherical window
from the entire celestial meridian

The Man with a Green Face

It was a beautiful morning
shoulder to shoulder
we watched the squadron sail out of sight
to the very end we believed
that a huge silence commanded
the sea of freedom and necessity
and that only illusions were real

Of course the squadron never returned
to any port   to any country
of course reality was an illusion
shoulder to shoulder
we scanned every mile of horizon
but freedom and necessity
were always within history—
only the man with a green face
tries to break out of history;
we let go of each other's shoulders
the beautiful morning shatters
between our dangling arms

We need more cunning to kill our hunger
more imagination to end our dreaming
we have to leave "we" behind
you won't find the man with a green face
in a group or a crowd
and if you say that only evil exists
then history will whisper back:
all great things are evil

Human House

I guess I'll be back late
I said and left the house
my house is made of words
an iceberg floats in my old wardrobe
unseen horizons wait in my bathroom
from my telephone: time, a whole desert
on the table: bread, salt, water
a woman lives in the water
hyacinths bloom from her eyeballs
of course she is metaphor herself
she changes the way words do
she's as free-form as a cat
I can't come near her name

I guess I'll be back late
no, no business meeting
not even a reunion
I ride ice trains
walk fluorescent underground arcades
cut across a shadowed square
ride in a mollusk elevator
violet tongues and gray lips in the trains
rainbow throats and green lungs underground
in the square, bubble language
foaming bubble information, informational information
adjectives, all the hollow adjectives
adverbs, paltry begging adverbs
and nouns, crushing, suffocating nouns
all I want is a verb

but I can't find one anywhere
I'm through with a society
built only of the past and future
I want the present tense

Because you open a door
doesn't mean there has to be a room
because there are windows
doesn't mean there's an interior
doesn't mean there's a space
where humans can live and die—
so far I've opened and shut
countless doors, going out each one
so I could come in through another
telling myself each time
what a wonderful new world lies just beyond
what do I hear?   from the paradise on the other side
dripping water
wingbeats
waves thudding on rocks
sounds of humans and beasts breathing
the smell of blood

Blood
it's been a while
I'd almost forgotten what it smells like
silence gathers around a scream
on the tip of a needle
as he walks slowly toward me
the surgeon puts on his rubber gloves
I close my eyes, open them again
things falling through my eyes
both arms spread like wings
hair streaming out full length
things descending momentary gaps of light
connecting darkness and darkness

I rise slowly from a table in a bar
not pulled by a political slogan or religious belief
it's hard enough trying to find my eyes
to see the demolition of the human house
the dismemberment of my language

My house, of course, isn't made of your words
my house is built of my words

Perhaps a Great Poem

A poem
rests, barely, on a single line
a kind of balance of terror
humans must hold out their arms
and endure this balance—
a moment's dizziness
will tilt your whole life

Perhaps a great poem
travels faster than the speed of light
forcing humans
to invade the present from the future
and the past from the present—
a dead man steps out of the ground,
returns to the hands of those who buried him,
then, back turned to them, continues on
to the flesh-colored dark that bore him,
the original birthing spring;
love moves from destruction toward completion
all things begin in their ending:
the permanent revolution
the withered-away state
a single poem

Perhaps a great poem is
in November light—
the light that pierces every object
making humans close their eyes,
stretch out their arms, stand precisely there

Every Morning After Killing Thousands of Angels

1

I read a boy's poem called
"Every Morning After Killing Thousands of Angels"
I forget the poem, but the title won't leave me
I drink some coffee
read a paper read by millions
all the misery
all the destruction in the world
herded into headlines and catch phrases
the only part I trust
is the financial page
a completely blank space governed
by the mechanics of capital and pure speculation

2

That boy's mornings
and my mornings—
how are they different?

3

But the boy can see the angels' faces

4

What do you do
after you kill them?

I go out walking

Where?

To a river with a very big bridge over it

Every morning?

Every morning
while my hands are still bloody

5

I can't kill thousands of angels
but I walk a dry path to the beach
the hot sky's still filled
with sweating typhoon clouds
the sea's a later color
fall is not summer at the horizon
narrow streams run through
spaces silted with darkness
weak-looking capillaries float on my thin hands:
no place to anchor a big bridge

6

Noon at this end of the bridge
everything shines
shirt buttons
decayed tooth
an air rifle

broken sunglass lens
pink shells
smells of seaweed
river water mixing with the sea
sand
and
as far
as my footprints

        7

It's my turn now
I'll tell you about the world
at the far end of the bridge
the shadow world
things and concepts totally shadow
shadows feeding on shadows
spreading, radiating like cancer cells
decomposing organs of drowned bodies
green thought swelling and distending
medieval markets surging with merchants and prostitutes and monks
cats, sheep, hogs, horses, cows
every kind of meat on the butcher shop hooks
but no blood anywhere

        8

So I can't see the bridge
unless I kill thousands of angels?

        9

What sight excites me most sexually?
the bridge has disappeared
a riderless black horse

crosses the world of light
slowly, toward the shadow world
but exhausted, it falls
crying animal tears but not rotting
gleaming directly to bone
pure white bone
and then to earth
and then
dawn comes
I've got to go out and live
after killing
killing thousands of angels

Things and Dreams

My sorrow was located
by an abstract bird
bird without qualities
without color or sound
bird in a silent movie
but at least it could fly
through my brain
around my stomach
at least it had wings
bird, what should I call you?
I wasn't a seer of visions
for four thousand days and nights—
I only tried to see them
          a small bird drops from the sky
that sky and that bird
were only abstractions
converging on plausible crossroads
where my heart might have stopped
was I alive? I held hard
to my sorrow until it broke
free and gave birth beneath
a simple color, simple sound

Footprints on the snow
and for the first time it lay there:
the world ruled by birds,
small animals, forest beasts—

squirrel tracks down an old elm
across the path
and into a wall of firs
no trace of momentary
hesitations, anxieties, judicious question marks

Foxprints stretch
up the valley path north of the village:
my hunger never left so straight a line

To escape abstractions I turned and began to track them instead. I
watched question marks and straight lines, but curves, what was
moving in curves? My fox feet tried to follow their blind, dancing
rhythms.

A small bird
prints clearer than its call
clawmarks sharper than its life
gashes of wingbeat on a rise of snow

Suddenly small things inside me become critics. Birds, insects, crawling
things, all aiming at the object I call "I."
In June. (I was over thirty.)

The bird's eyes are evil itself
it watches without judging
the bird's tongue is evil itself
it swallows without judging

Fragment of the number 6, continuing —

Sharply split tongue of a starred dove
flicking spear of a great spotted woodpecker
sculpting-knife tongue of a woodcock
soft cutter in the mouth of a golden thrush

I began writing poems
wanting only a bird's
trembling tongue
but the tongue became concrete
a starred dove, a great spotted woodpecker, a woodcock, a golden thrush,
    and, to be fair, aggressive, reactionary bugs

Piece of the number 9.

Paths of death and sex,
of small animals and insects
a band of bees bends and scatters—
thousands of needles lying in ambush

Notified of my sorrow by thousands of needles. But would I ever hear of
    happiness? Then, suddenly, things are.
People produce things, and these made things create people. And their
    happiness. In these liaisons, our thingly human culture.
Things answer by the law of perspective. We're forced to look at things
    close to us with eyes that see to the horizon.
Yet I must live among them: occupy that name, that detail, that light,
    that darkness. My legs take me toward The Farm.
Done in oils in 1921–22.
"This painting," he said, "reproduces everything I knew in my village,
    even the footprints."
The Farm has completely repealed the law of perspective. But the more
    you love things the more another law enacts itself.
First, the interval between the wall of the farmhouse and the frame of the
    barn. In it, birds, small animals, livestock, a child, a naked child, his
    outline cut out with sharp scissors like a paper figure from a certain
    dreampoint and fixed along the blue plane of the sky, holding up in
    the center a tall black tufted tree with a sinewed trunk—an olive?
Catalonia.
Dream nourished by the deep purple earth.
It resists all purely human movements, all the exchange rates of history.

Refusing temporal perspective,
everything exists equally: plow, pump, wagon, ladder, bucket, sprinkler,
    snake, lizard, snail, humans, corn, chickens, cocks, rabbits, dogs,
    pigeons, mules.
Supporting this refusal: the earth and underground springs and seeping
    pockets of poems, all moving to violent rhythms.
The root of The Farm's dream was exposed to history, to the crisis that
    deepened in 1922. In the next fifteen years the Civil War brought
    him to Catalonian light, to voices slanting back through Rome to
    ancient Greece, to the dream republic, the commonwealth that
    existed equally with the deep purple earth.
The Dream City, The Communal Dream, The Farm. Prosed by Franco.
During World War II he produced the Constellations series with André
    Breton. From occupied Paris to Barcelona, then to Majorca.
After the war he fell into the dream again, with lithographs, ceramics,
    stone and fire and earth,
grasping after every kind of material and subject.
Wall surfaces.
Rocks.
Copper.
Canvas.
And then.
Earth and
sky.

After peace was declared
he was attacked
by the light and rhythm
called happiness.
His name? Joan Miró.
His first book was published in 1940 in Japan by Takiguchi Shūzō.
Thirty years later Takiguchi put out a book of poems illustrated by Miró,
    Handmade Proverbs.
The first poem

    Bones of the mirror back to back, flesh becoming light

    Your eye, your hand, your breast . . .
    you're one of twins

One clear day a bird dived into the ground, crying
        there was another world in this one

Insomniac stone, lifted in sudden wind,
stone's other self. Night, quickly.

Someone? Clarity, speak in things!
Eternity dries up with night,
flows with water.

Another world doesn't flinch from this one.
Toward it, on a fair day,
face the stone mirror
        that is Miró
and fly into it.
Probably, unlike the bird,
you won't succeed in killing yourself.
But surely
we will
change lives.

Dissolving Mountain

The top of the sun
clears the edge of a wide, grassy plain
birds, so many taken by the sky
crows in flocks   vultures motionless
on the bank
stone steps slant into the Ganges
naked human bodies writhe
human because they are naked
when they (including me, of course) put on their clothes
they step once more beyond the human
young women enter the river still wrapped in brightly colored cotton, long
    black hair spreading out in the current   they rinse their mouths with
    the brown water, float crimson and yellow flowers out to the gods of the
    Himalayas
men in loincloths submerge completely   when they finally reappear they
    smear their bodies with sacred ashes   they clean their loincloths by
    slapping them on the steps, squeezing the remaining water into their eyes
    and mouths
water brown with excrement and muck
carries jasmine petals and the carcass of a calf
slowly toward the Bay of Bengal
when I open my eyes again
I am crossing the plain on a long-distance bus
mist, still thick at midday
hides the whole plateau, 5,300 feet above sea level
finally the bus stops at the edge of a volcanic crater
the mist clears and we are surrounded by sulfur gas

we
the middle-aged driver and I and the gray bus
and a woman's voice from a tape deck
describing how the air above the crater
is so sulfurous no bird can fly it

Then what is that?
a single bird   or shaped like a bird
rustling against the wind
birdlike shape
submerged in sulfur

The driver takes a deep breath
and pushes the gearshift

Green Conceptual Body

Dogs run inside dogs
cats sleep inside cats
birds fly inside birds nailed to the sky
fish swim inside fish across deserts and pant in water

But people can't run inside inner people
so they run inside conceptual bodies
they can't dream free-form cat dreams
so they watch insomniac dreams
they can't swim like fish
so they labor to float concepts
and they can't fly like birds
so they put wings on concepts
to feel the pleasure of crashing

Sometimes people
are inside rooms
but they never live
inside people (inside bodies)
people sleep inside different concepts,
choose vegetables over meat,
boil, fry, make eating a chore;
concepts peer into the blood,
make people need forks and chopsticks
people even need shovels to bury corpses
stopping to lick ice cream as they work

People go out walking
on nice days in early summer
leaving the people inside themselves in their rooms;
these shut-in bodies measure their blood pressure and spoon out honey
and lead thoughts across their voices;
what does the spirit, shut in, do?
what went out walking
weren't bodies, weren't spirit
were conceptual bodies with legs
they built the vertical nightmare of medieval Gothic
the ascending nightmare knotting heaven and earth
invisible ropes
hierarchical classes
wings for angels
ivory horns for devils
the materials had to be combustible
the dream irreversible

I walk a small path through the field
and come out by the Tama River
on the other side two men tend fishing lines
no conceptual bodies: people
drowsy, I lie down in the grass — that instant
the vertical axis swings, the horizontal
pushes through my conceptual body
the Gothic collapses
voluptuous curves and colors spurt out
the smell of water comes this far

Sun directly overhead
objects but no shadows
my conceptual body turns cat-indeterminate
its footsteps
utterly soundless

Leaving one dream to enter another,
you can hardly call that waking;

I have no Globe to world
my thoughts to actors on a stage —
I'd rather look, for a split-second,
at the most modern nightmare, nuclear war
but the moment I saw it
because I had come to the edge of the field
they would be watching me: eyes in
angelic missiles and beautiful hydrogen bombs;
I'm not a passerby, not a spectator
I myself am the nightmare

All I still want
is, on the tongues of gravediggers,
the taste of ice cream

Harbor Marie

Born in 1921, still a prostitute
she's not a former office worker, former college student
working to buy a car, a trip to Europe,
to own a restaurant, even to remodel her body
Harbor Marie's a real prostitute
probably the last prostitute in Japan;
after antibiotics wiped out syphilis and TB
there could be no more poets, philosophers or military geniuses
there's no way a real prostitute can get along
these days the younger women
care only about their bankbooks

Underneath thick makeup
her face is covered with wrinkles
a glacier photographed from a satellite
her Ice Age began when Japan lost the war
she moved from a watch store glittering
on the Ginza down to Yokohama
and then to the U.S. Navy base in Yokosuka
she lived in the U.S. inside Japan
her customers were officers
trained at Harvard and at Princeton
she was brought in twenty-three times
in thirty-six years, but her record's clean
according to a detective from Kanagawa
who was in kindergarten when she started working

She married a Japanese, then an American
but she's single now

"I guess I'll be alone even when I die."
she lived twenty-eight years in the U.S.
inside Japan, and now
"I don't live anywhere now."
she and everyone in the industrialized world—
our peace is a hostage to future crisis
our peace is a drug for fear
only wars, uprisings, terrorism can numb us to it
we are all boat people
and when we finally make it to shore
infinity of glaciers
Harbor Marie

A friend, a young warehouse guard in Yokohama
met an amazing old woman one morning
in the cheap restaurant where he eats.
A fall wind was already blowing, but all
she wore was an old, thin after-bath kimono.
She tottered on her feet
and put down two whole bowls of rice.
That night my friend went down to the docks
to a bar called Erotica for some cheap brandy.
Three or four half-naked women were working hard
to get the regulars, Greek sailors off a Panamanian freighter,
to finish their small beers in less than two hours
so they loved the way he poured down his brandy.
He, out of love as usual, was soon
in the mood for a good walk, and there
out in the mist under a lamppost
in a black suit and pearl necklace
stood a beautiful prostitute, alone

"I don't live anywhere now."

My Imperialism

I sink into bed
on the first Monday after Pentecost
and bless myself
since I'm not a Christian

Yet my ears still wander the sky
my eyes keep hunting for underground water
and my hands hold a small book
describing the grotesqueness of modern white society
when looked down at from the nonwhite world
in my fingers there's a thin cigarette —
I wish it were hallucinogenic
though I'm tired of indiscriminate ecstasy

Through a window in the northern hemisphere
the light moves slowly past morning to afternoon
before I can place the red flare, it's gone:
darkness

Was it this morning that my acupuncturist came?
a graduate student in Marxist economics, he says he changed
to medicine to help humanity, the animal of animals, drag itself peacefully to its
    deathbeds
forty years of Scotch whiskey's roasted my liver and put me
into the hands of a Marxist economist
I want to ask him about *Imperialism, A Study* —
what Hobson saw in South Africa at the end of the nineteenth century
may yet push me out of bed

even if you wanted to praise imperialism
there aren't enough kings and natives left
the overproduced slaves had to become white

Only the nails grow
the nails of the dead grow too
so, like cats, we must constantly
sharpen ours to stay alive
Only The Nails Grow—not a bad epitaph
when K died his wife buried him in Fuji Cemetery
and had To One Woman carved on his gravestone
true, it was the title of one of his books
but the way she tried to have him only
to herself almost made me cry
even N, who founded the modernist magazine *Luna*
while Japan prepared to invade China
got sentimental after he went on his pension;
F, depressed
S, manic, builds house after house
A has abdominal imperialism: his stomach's colonized his legs
M's deaf, he can endure the loudest sounds;
some people have only their shadows grow
others become smaller than they really are
our old manifesto had it wrong: we only looked upward
if we'd really wanted to write poems
we should have crawled on the ground on all fours—
when William Irish, who wrote *The Phantom Lady*, died
the only mourners were stock brokers
Mozart's wife was not at his funeral

My feet grow warmer as I read
Kōtoku Shūsui's *Imperialism, Monster of the Twentieth Century*, written back in
    1901
when he was young N wrote "I say strange things"
was it the monster that pumped tears from his older eyes?

Poems are commodities without exchange value

but we're forced to invade new territory
by crises of poetic overproduction

We must enslave the natives with our poems
all the ignorant savages under sixty
plagued by a surplus of clothes and food—
when you're past sixty
you're neither a commodity
nor human

Dialog on an Intersection and a Missing Line

When I start to write a poem my hand trembles   like the tongue of
a small bird

You've already written poems   about small birds' trembling tongues
wasn't your hand trembling   while you wrote them?

But I wasn't conscious of my hand then   I didn't know what a hand
meant   I thought you heard poems with your eyes   saw them with
your ears

Well, what are they   those thin hands of yours?

These?   they don't mean anything special   they haven't
strangled anyone   haven't even shaken hands with a leper

You mean   all they've held are whiskey glasses?

Maybe   well, they've also scooped up a little, just a little, earth and
ash   they can't handle fire and water

What about women?

They haven't been overly ardent   they don't like spongy things
flaccid things   soft, wet things

Are you gay?

They dislike men even more   males   conceptual, aggressive, weak   their weakness makes them neurotic and self-centered

How about humans   humanity?

Interesting   nothing else in the world is so amusing   the other
animals are too accurate   they never make mistakes   whales, sheep,
bulbuls, they never laugh the way humans do   of course humans
    don't laugh at the sun, say, or the moon   humans only laugh at
humans

Amazing how they do it   on only two legs

They do fall down sometimes   even trip over words as if they were
stones   last March   I was walking across an intersection in Delhi
    a bus had stopped and an old man was getting off   just then   this
white-haired Indian man tripped and fell   flat on his back, kicking his
dark, skinny legs around and around   I'd just arrived in Delhi from
Tokyo   and was wandering through the intersection   it was noon
and the sun was unbearably hot   Indians in crowds of white robes
    a world without shadows   for a moment   everything stopped
moving   then something in my stomach moved   up through my
throat   a rush of laughter   I had no idea what was so funny   but
it was, incredibly funny

What happened to the old man?

Someone helped him up, of course   he cursed a little   then
disappeared down a crowded street   even so   I don't know what was
so funny

But if you'd been   in Shinjuku or Ginza   you'd have walked
right by   if you'd been in Delhi for a while   you wouldn't even have
bothered to look   but you're just in from Tokyo   the world is upside
down   at that moment an old man falls from a bus   his long dark legs
and white robe   and your hand begins to tremble

So you think my hand trembles   from spasms of laughter?

Your hand saw it   saw the world not world   because we try to
see with our eyes   or tell ourselves we see with our eyes   we end up
in unthinkable places   the way you were crossing that Delhi intersection

Yes   not a shadow anywhere   the sun directly above

Your hand   is crossing a dream   after the poem's missing line

Iijima Kōichi

Iijima Kōichi

by Tsuruoka Yoshihisa

Iijima Kōichi was born on February 25th, 1930. His boyhood was deeply affected by the war. When on December 8th (J.T.), 1941, Japan started the war with a surprise attack on Pearl Harbor, Iijima was in the third year of high school (under the old system) and he joined those mobilized to work in a shipyard producing parts for special-purpose submarines. In 1945 he took and passed the examination to enter the Military Flying Academy, but in August of the same year Japan lost the war. Iijima returned to his native Okayama, then in ruins after enemy air-raids, to resume his high school life there. The awakening and establishment of his self-identity thus took place in the midst of wartime disorder.

Iijima started writing poems in earnest around 1946 (he was reading Baudelaire and Supervielle then), and the first collection of his poems entitled *Strangers' Sky* came out in 1953. The war still is strongly felt in this volume, written during the last years of his adolescence. The fireweeds growing among the ruins excite fellow-feeling in him, but he is skeptical about the energetic reconstruction that soon starts all over Japan. Superficial and statistical prosperity does not inspire him. ". . . I only have words to cope with this. I can only build cities with words. That is the reason for my poetry" — Iijima is to write later looking back on his first years as a poet. What to seek is "total freedom", through words, in contradistinction to the "false" prosperity and freedom that have replaced fascism.

> Soon we shall learn to recognize a sound.
> In that small sound when a vessel touches another.
> In that sound when a wind walks away.

103

In that sound when an oar cleaves the water.
In that sound inside our selves.

Look in it for a road.
Look in it for a woman's face.
The roads are without number.
But we shall choose one and no other.

"Road"

This poem from *Strangers' Sky* clearly defines Iijima's stance toward the world around him. Just as the decision to start the war was made by others in his ignorance, postwar Japan almost totally alienates him. What his mind still recalls is that sky and that sun above those ruins of 1945, and he listens eagerly for a small sound there in order to discover a new "road". His poetry reveals this search for that "road".

In 1955 Iijima encountered surrealism, and the next year he joined other contemporary poets (Ōoka Makoto among others) to form a surrealism society. He personally knew Takiguchi Shūzō (a prominent Japanese surrealist who had been active from before the war and in direct contact with André Breton), which perhaps bore a part in bringing him to surrealism. Iijima's yearning after that white-heated summer sun in the face of postwar realities linked itself directly to surrealism which sought to liberate living and thinking totally from all containment. *Five Poems At An Hour Before Dawn and Other Poems* (pub. 1967) is the result of the above union.

Infinitesimal roses
Infinitesimal sand
Infinitesimal impossibilities
Infinitesimal stalks
Will there be an infiltration
Of those things
Into other infinitesimal
Roses, sand, impossibilities, stalks. . .?

In this collection we constantly meet a consciousness attempting to keep itself at a distance by means of automatic writing. Here words acquire the hardness of things so as to break themselves of the traditional lyricism of Japanese poetry (*tanka* and *haiku*). Difficult as it must have been, Iijima's surrealist technique has enabled him to effect this separation from lyricism. What is more, even humor begins to appear in his poetry now:

104

. . .
In my already funereal dominion
Erect
One
Pure
Transparent city.

To build a "transparent city" is just what *An Esquisse on the Private Ownership System* (pub. 1970) does with its perfect language. With Iijima "seeing" is always equated to the restoration of hope, and this logic further develops into the art of "seeing the invisible." The volume harvests a series of poems entitled "The Visible" which begins as follows:

The geographies I pursued alone in my dreams
Must be committed to paper. . .

If attaching importance to dreams is equivalent to contemplating the invisible, keeping accounts of those dreams will be comparable to forcing the invisible to materialize on paper.

. . .
A sea urchin moves
A sea urchin moves
A volcano exists
For a split second a volcano   rocks
Across a camp dripping with sweat
A volcano moves
A volcano moves
Misery moves
Misery exists
Or it does not. . .

The mushy red substance inside a sea urchin exists, and is visible, just like the lava, the undulating magma, inside a live volcano. The visible and the invisible are linked here, or, in other words, reality and dreams correspond. Such is the world presented by Iijima's poetry. And if a volcano "moves" so does misery. Here nature (volcano) and human existence (misery) are both defined as visible. In this manner Iijima's poetry focuses on the visible as a synthesis of reality and non-reality. At this subtle junction of reality and nonreality Iijima keeps spinning his poems, carefully avoiding clear-cut conclusions: each of his poems is at once a testimony to hope and an act of fate.

Goya's First Name? (1974), *Barcelona* (1976), *Miyako* (1979), *Wander Up and Down In Ueno and Penetrate Ōu* (1980)—Iijima has been publishing substantial volumes one after another. In the first two books mentioned above the main theme is the poet's trip to Spain. Miyako, Ueno, and Ōu are all place names; in the latter two books as well travel constitutes the main subject. The "walking" or "moving" rhythm has always been the bottom current in all of Iijima's poems ever since *Strangers' Sky*: his attitude toward reality and dreams seems to be furnished with this rhythm as its basic, built-in mechanism. In all of the four books above that have come out of his mature years Iijima is always spurred by a sort of wanderlust, an impulse to start on a journey which is another form of "walking." Perhaps to be on the move serves the practical purpose of shoving him out of his occasional mental depressions, besides offering him new aspects of reality.

> The memory of walking   persists
> Inside my body.
> Whom am I to tell
> About this walking in my dreams?
>
> The memory of something that can never be told in words
> This body keeps
> But in what depth?
> Such a consciousness is   perhaps   time.
>
>   "The Memory of Walking"

The journeys that Iijima makes are but instances of "this walking in (his) dreams." When he writes poems he is attempting to say the unsayable, performing an act of exorcism for the well-being of his body and mind. Somewhere in the notes attached to *Miyako*, Iijima tells us that in Okinawa a magical formula ("*ishigandō*") is often inscribed on stone walls for the purpose of charming away evil spirits. Perhaps Iijima's poems, too, are each of them "*ishigandō*."

Iijima has published a large number of essays on a variety of subjects—French as well as Japanese men of letters, surrealism, art, cinema and so on. He has recently started writing novels as well. We certainly have much to look forward to from this so richly gifted poet.

106

Iijima Kōichi
The Poems

America Symphony

Where we were "mobilized for labor" we used to sit
On our heels in a dug-out shelter. We listened to Jazz.
For the first time. From a wretched portable radio
Outlandish melodies came *gatagata*.
Up above a shiny silver speck — a B29 — went *kiin*
The sky was a perfect blue: we saw
That speck purely as object.

The object showered us with incendiaries & machine gun bullets.
That was the end of our war & the end too of
Boiled barley with rice reeking of Bakelite.
The object came down at Atsugi
&from it trooped out lots of GIs.
The object spat out human beings.
The human beings that came out of the object were
Gay goodhearted Yankees.
We read "A Farewell to Arms" for the first time:
Savoring that title so good to our ears.
Popeye ate spinach as before.
In the films the object also spat out
America was busy eating walking & loving.

Fifteen years since then has seen much happen
Between us & America. Now we can
Easily picture the sergeants & sergeant majors

Not much different from us—human beings—
On board the flying objects
Okinawa——Pearl Harbor——Guadalcanal——bloody
Place names still fastened
Between us & America
But with rusted pins now.
Handbills shouting "American Imperialists Go Home"
Were washed & scrubbed away—
Bygones now.
The muddy rivulet beneath Sukiyabashi Bridge was filled in:
No more US marines to be thrown in there in the middle of winter.
All the same—objects still squeak across the sky, still
Turning the Braun tube images on our TV screens into waves
&giving us nerves. How hot how much rain & how noisy the cicadas
In the summer of that surrender year—now gone clean out of our minds.
But I still clearly remember
Hurried footsteps up & down the stairs,
Whispering
&light suddenly flooding our rooms
Finally freed from blackout curtains.
How the sea of sunflowers looked like moonlight.
Father came back from a remote mining town
Carrying a beggar's bag on his back, looking black
&exhausted like everybody else. In time he smiled
As if driven to the end of all his wits.
What was I thinking then? About my poor self completely deprived
Of all sense of balance by an aviation-aptitude testing machine?
About the dusty white narrow rows of houses of Kyoto & their low eaves?
Or about the wormwood colored Korean factory boys
Standing in groups in front of an empty warehouse?
The war that ended like a kite whose string suddenly snaps—

Where had it been blown away to now? What was to happen now?
America, that's how lost we were the day you won the war.

Now your Eisenhower is to pay a visit to Japan to celebrate
The centennial of Japan & US friendship. Shall we
Greet the flying object when it lands at Haneda with stars
&stripes in our left hands & little rising suns in our right?
The Japanese government will give the biggest feast ever.
Most of the Japanese people will just watch—with no
Profundity of emotion their eyes will simply recognize
The brave enemy general of the Second World War.
We too will watch. In the rising dust
Our protesting fists will blur.
To act
Has always been someone else's business.
Always someone else's.
Diapers & nylons hang on clotheslines—again today
The murky duralumin sea glitters beyond.
The sea of objects.

Cut-Out Sky

She has been storing
Aspects of the sky that I have not known.
In her memory
She has several such pieces cut out of the sky.

Sometimes she comes upstairs
&gives them to me
Carefully, one by one.

There is a marsh in the sky,
&it is inhabited
By various creatures, she says.

There is a school child, for example, squatting down
On his heels at a small station built of wood.
She has passed by the station only once,
&the child is carrying a slipper-bag in his hand.

Next she said—
Among pieces of the sky now lost
There have been much clearer ones.

Streams & Rivers

1

You have no large river
Inside you;
That is the ultimate explanation
Of your sorry plight.

I dare say
Your misery is attributable
To the absence of a large river
Inside you.

2

I saw a river just once
This last summer.
One day at Ohizumi I got on a train
Heading for Seibuchichibu, away from Ikebukuro.
It was still morning.
There were only a few passengers in each car.
Wind came in from open windows.
That was the only time I enjoyed coolness
This last summer.
A river appeared to meander
Among the mountains.
It went on & on without end.
It was an authentic river
Running just for its own sake.
That river

Was the most noble entity
I saw this last summer.

3

That river
Crosses my mind from time to time
These days. Rivers
Have been haunting me.
For a long time I haven't met persons
Who have a river inside,
Much less any
Who have a large river inside.

4

Water
Quenches thirst.
But there is a kind of thirst
That can't be quenched.
That kind of thirst
Exists indomitably
&accompanies you
Everywhere.

5

In the summer of 1945
You were in the town of N to which you had moved for safety.
In the garden of Mr S's main house (there were such things as main houses
    then)
You were in the company of Mr S & his nurses,
All gathered in front of a radio
As the Emperor decreed surrender.

Everybody was tongue-tied

Only the sky above was shining.
We couldn't bear to look at
Each other's faces.
Unable to either cry or laugh —
As the phrase goes.

Suddenly
Dr S told his wife to go & draw out
All the money from the bank.
Mr S's words at that time
Lingered long
In my ears
As something unpleasant.
But now I think otherwise:
The postwar days of Japan
Started running at full speed
In the direction of Mr S's words.

6

It must have been the 17th or the 18th of that August
I got on a train & went to where the Tenth Foot was quartered
To have a look at the barracks & walk around the walls.
The place looked completely deserted:
No sign of life.
Except on telephone poles and walls by the gate
Those posters that said "All-Out War!"

7

Stations smell.
I have never known anything that had a worse smell
Than the stations in the 20th year of Showa,
Year of the Surrender.
When pushed to the wall

Even beautiful women start smelling like that.

8

I don't remember any more
What I was doing in those days.
I remember the brightness of the river
Only a few minutes walk
From where I lived.

9

One thing was heavy
On my mind.
On August 10th I received a telegram
Telling me to join the Army Aviation Academy
On August 12th.
I figured I no longer had to,
But then I could not ignore the order either, could I?
No need to go now,
But I kind of wanted to go:
My first dilemma after the war.
Thirty years since then
Have found me in similar dilemmas
Without a break.

10

In the summer of 1939
I went with my brother to see the Kinoshita Circus.
Elephants. . .A honky-tonk called "Nature" or something.
The flying trapeze, tight rope walking,
Clowns. . .the big tall tents;
The only things in your country that are a match for cathedrals
Are those tents.

When tents were hoisted in a field
We were ecstatic both going and returning.
The smells of animals, the heated atmosphere, the dripping sweat
Crackers, caramels, cold coffee. . .
Above all the smell of those elephants, lions & monkeys. . .
The smell of urine boiled dry by the sun.
(Circuses have no smell
On television)
You were a fourth grader.
Your brother is always a little too wild.
The Kinoshita Circus smacks of the Sino-Japanese War.

11

Television is over summer is over
There is nothing more to think about.
Think then about Mishima Yukio.
In the evening of the day Mishima died on a high veranda
You were meeting a lady
From Nice,
An old lady who is always sprightly
And knows Japan quite well,
In a hotel room at Ohmori,
Well lit but somehow bleak,
She looked tired & dark—the first time I had ever
Seen her tired & somber.
—The way Mishima died, she said
&looked all the more somber.
She showed me some Piccaso woodcuts,
But even Picasso looked gloomy there.
When we were about to part
She gave me a photograph of herself & Picasso
Smiling with their arms around each other's shoulders—
She was much younger in the photo & very proud of it.

You did not like Mishima so much
While he was still alive:
You think a lot about him
Now
That he is gone.

He used to go on television
In a white cambric suit,
And offer us forced martial laughter.
But I'm sure he must have hated television.
He must have found unbearable
This emptiness after television.
I believe I know very well how he must have felt.

He did live in a gorgeous Western-style house,
But that was imitation West;
Even his military uniform was fake.
He was always feeling inferior
To the absolutely genuine élitism
Of the Meiji poet Ohgai.
He put on a fake military uniform,
Waged a fight against all television
& destroyed himself.
(I might respect but would not like at all
Anybody who is incapable of self-destruction.)
He must have wanted to make
Everyday a New Year's Day.
Poor fellow.

But perhaps you like Mishima better
Than anybody else who is involved
In something like literature now.

After Mishima's death

You went mad little by little.
You couldn't bear to look at anyone else's face.

If you hate televion
You cannot survive today.
(Those moments-after-moments when you forced yourself
To learn to watch television)
All Japan is comatose
In front of television sets.

12

Poetry is desperately trying
To keep itself going despite television.
(Desperately is not a word
You like much.)
As you patiently crouch .in the virulence of summer
You understand that very well.

13

Thinking of going
To see the river again.
Impossible to think of more
Than that now.
Better
To think of a river
Than to think of blood.
On a train again this windy day,
Windows all closed, stuffy.
Saddened to think there will never be Japanese
"Thought" worthy of the name.
You love now
Only the tragic dead.

Bokokugo (Native Language)

During the half year I was abroad
I did not feel like writing poems
Even once
I was busy walking around
Oblivious of myself
When asked why I was not writing poems
I never could give a good answer

Now back in Japan
I just have to write poems
Only now am I beginning to understand
That half year
I was busy just walking around
Not writing poems—
It is that I am now back
Into my own *bokokugo*

Inside the word *bokokugo*
Are "mother country" & "language"
During that half year when I was telling myself
That I was cut off from my mother & country & language
I could walk through reality
Immune to harm—

There was hardly any need
For me to write poems

In April Paul Celan
Threw himself into the Seine & died
I believe I can understand that act
Of that poet who was a Jew
Poetry is a sad thing
Poetry is said to put one's national language right
But for me it is not so
Daily I am injured inside my own *bokokugo*
Every night I have to set out
For another *bokokugo*
That is what makes me write poems
Keeps me going

St. Paul de Vence

On top of a hillock in St. Paul de Vence
You are talking now with a lady
About Jacques Prévert
She wanted Prévert
To write good poems
&tried to give him fine Japanese paper
But Prévert said he wrote poems on toilet paper
&declined her offer
Such a wicked person isn't he
But such a fine such an excellent poet
It seems that Jacques Prévert
No longer comes to St. Paul de Vence

Poetry and Catching Catfish

I used to have fun catching catfish   as a child
The other day   I remembered that suddenly
In the darkness of a tunnel   the catfish
Would be hiding
There
The tunnel was a little lower than a grownup's height
Your voice would echo so
Into your net   the fish   would come jumping
A splash   a thump   &a fish in your net
That sensation
Was so alive   in the very navel of your day
(That catfish catching
Was contemporaneous with history
I now know
Say the civil wars   or
The Polish post office incident in Danzig)
Today I   don't catch catfish
But write poems instead
Only   do I
Love the world now
As much as I did then?

The expansion of the world   &the question of one's place in it
Those children so lost in catching catfish
Space-time enveloped them so gently once
The world left them   alone

Curiously Enough Affinity Grows

Curiously enough, things begin to look alike.
That is a good sign.
As the colors of a forest melt in the rain
As the hot & cool temperatures are shared so readily
By two lovers sitting next to each other
So, little by little, things begin
To flow into one another.
Such a time will come.
It will come
To those who wish for it
With the certainty
Of branches that attract birds.
If it does not come, that is because
It is not beckoned.

Similitude develops.
The color of life,
Enkindled, glows
& similitude grows.
The color of life will not desist.
It blends & thereby attains perfection.
The black of pain & sorrow even will come
To uphold the yellow, red & blue dance of joy.
Affinity increases.

It begins to look like a woman.
A woman
Begins to look like everything else.

In the whirlpool of affinity
The past with its wry face
Loses its pursuer's certificate.
The empty expanse of night
Begins, willy-nilly, to grope for tomorrow's breath.
The world is richer now than before
In the form of one woman
Who, already, is beautiful
Lips, gentle hands & eyes that can
Embrace me, turn me
Face to face with a large deep lake.
Her small throat
Trembles now
Like a bulb that pushes a flower open,
& the sputum that runs over from inside her throat
Flaps its wings, spins light
& becomes tens of thousands of birds.
Next the down-covered hearts of those birds
Go through so many changes to become
Throbbing bulbs.

Curiously enough, kinship spreads.
That is a good sign.
If it does not come, then that is because
It is not beckoned.
Her lake tells me to dream
Of that which is still afar off,
Traps me in its laughter, makes to stop me
From going any farther

& melts my heart which is inclined to be frozen.
We meet on almost fictional streets,
Streets teeming, moreover, with this terrible
Cruelty & gentleness,
Streets extremely hilarious & unhappy
Where din & silence live right next to each other.
Streets where the direct echoes of
The tens of thousands of voices of Budapest & Portside
Slaughtered by 'pirates' & 'gangsters'
Threaten us without a break.
Streets where window cleaners are seen
Pulling themselves up the faces of buildings by their creaking ropes hand over hand.

I agree to believe in one thing.
What more should I believe in?
In order to fill up the long-standing despair,
In order to satisfy the long-standing fiction of our broken hearts,
One night,
One morning
Its clean air
The surprise-attack of a blue sky,
&one encounter fresh & intense
Like gasoline running over,
That's enough.

What Words Are to Us

1

Cheeks dappled by the sun
Our gestures
Still resemble those of refugees.
Hungry eyes become us,
Dry mouth still becomes us well.

Underneath a remote sky
The illusion of an arsenal disintegrates.
The illusion of a future city disintegrates.
The image that becomes visible
On a warping pyrograph.

We are not yet accustomed
To paying our respects to the dead.
We do not catch on to fear.
We are not able to quantify
How much space words will uphold.

Memory associates itself with things unmade;
Words too collect nothing but fragments.
Our field of vision—
A mirror that reflects nothing

Looking out on a plain scattered with dead bugs.

The search to locate a 'place',
A magnetic field where scattering images converge
Is an activity of—the mind?
The line of vision sustained by a hundred refugees—
The constellation of a hundred people.

"The eyes of refugees uphold this century."

2

Words have no flags to hoist.
As we tried to mirror our own selves
On the surface of words
No trembling daybreak sky appeared there;
No flicker of the future city we saw there.

Who crouches
Silently hugging the knees?
The residuum of our ancesters' dreams
Proffered behind the upper arms of people
Or in the depth of their eye-sockets?
Or is it our own peaceful blood?
Are we the ones to arrive last of all?
Or do we stand here before anybody else?
We would be a party to the void,
We would malign those walking now,
If we answered the question without hesitation.

3

An attempt
To etch words on the sky.
On the Tahitian sky   on the sky over a dry land

On the sky above foamy breakers
People have been walking, with burdens on their backs

Trying to catch fish at the water's edge
Using trees for tents. We too
Step into the line. Will the bird's wings flap?
Will springs run over inside people?
Did waterfalls look for entrances?
Our clumsy song begins there,
Crouches there with the severed head of an ox.
It will conduct our own going.
Words that resemble so much the fragments of a cloudy sky.
An attempt to etch words on the sky.

December, 1959

I'd like to write a poem long as a roller bandage, put it round my neck
Cure my influenza. That's the only thing we can do in December
In this metropolis where it's so easy to catch cold.
We who unlike Fascists have no plans to make
What can we do?
Just crowd each other here?
In the year 1886 Berlin, Baden, Koblenz
&Hamburg were also crowded with cabs, & a poet
Who worked as a tutor & was suffering from a heart disease wrote
"We would very much like to be *them*
On the other side of the glass panels of the aquarium.
They dream their dreams right there
Where they were born & right there in their own excrement
They stay put & make love."

At the coffee stand in front a girl in a duster works
Until evening, until her hair is all loose & dry.
She sells a drink that has the same color & taste year in & year out.
Inside the dark building another girl of about the same age
Operates the elevator & she keeps saying
"Third floor, fourth floor" nine to five.
We feel we are their compatriots afflicted with the same trachoma.
I've just come up the stairs from a basement room with people
In wornout overcoats, from an old film in which there were scenes
In a morgue. A man, his name & address unknown, his height

A hundred & seventy-three centimeters, a birthmark
On his face, was lying in a wooden box. He was still unidentified
When he was put in an elevator with an iron railing for a door
& was all very quietly taken to the first floor.

December winds are cold. Our decomposing rhymes too
Are bleak.
Shall we speak up here & call somebody
A few names as loudly as we can?
Will that warm us up?
We too would like to sing beside a redhot burning stove
In our human voice. But we
Cannot sing in our natural voice—we have
Influenza. In order to express ourselves we have to
Dip our pens
In freezing ink.

Shining Circles

I like to go round a prismatic interior like an aquarium
Or to clamber up a tower & then down
And to come back to the old entrance/exit
At exhibitions the world images that you follow crawlingly
Will come full circle
Circuses have their smell, animals & gyrations in the air
In Federico Fellini movies there are tours of the Hell
Purifying caves, secret passages, white plastered woman & the crackle of jesters
I'm always in quest there of the world's vagina, the earth's navel

My ambulations describe a circle which will bring me
Back to the old entrance/exit hundreds & thousands of times
I even opt to run around inside my own nightmares
To be on the move, on the run
To be made sport of by marvel
To be pushed around—
These are doings of my own choosing

Aquariums, exhibitions, circuses & festivals
Everything in our country is no better than a miniature garden
Shivering in poverty-stricken light
No hope for anything electrifying

Like the sparkling bubbles of brass wind boiling over
Even in movie houses people don't laugh much

All the same—in this age of white collars when people are more alienated from
           one another than ever before
I seem to want to go round & round inside shining circles
Like aquariums and towers where rogues, drunks, jesters,
Frenzy, & white-plastered madwomen thrive

Tada Chimako

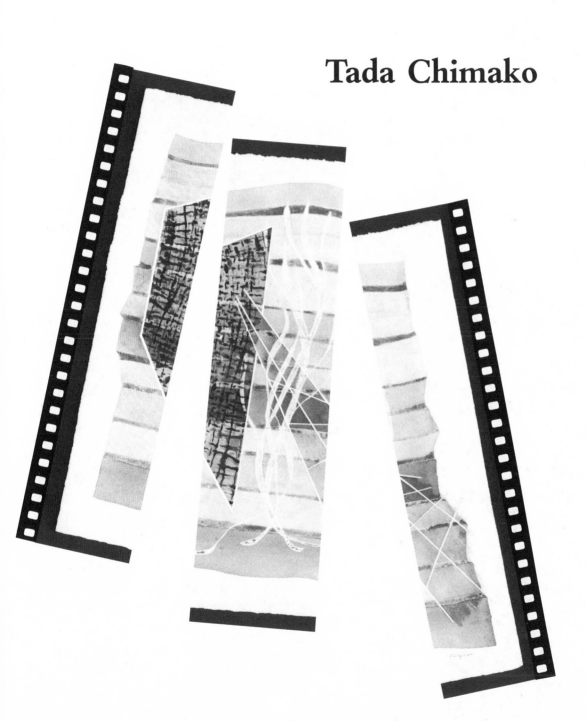

Tada Chimako

by Ōoka Makoto

In modern Japan it has sometimes been disastrous to be called an "intellectual poet." This is especially true for women poets, whom Japanese society has long preferred as writers of confessions drawn from only the most personal, non-intellectual experiences—love affairs and the like.

There also has existed in this country since very early times a somewhat primitive cult-of-nature which European Romanticism, since its introduction into Japan in the late nineteenth century, has tended to reinforce in its contempt for any trace of intellect in poetry. In this view, a powerful flow of spontaneous emotion is the hallmark of the pure and the natural, "the True." Intellect is merely an obstruction, intrusive and suspect. Poetry and intelligence, so closely intertwined during the classical period of Japanese literature, now become two separate, even hostile concepts, and the term "intellectual poet" a kind of insult. There is a tacit understanding among poets, critics, and the public that an intellectual poet lacks some necessary measure of sincerity in the realm of emotion.

But intellectual poets are not, of course, automatically inferior and negligible. Like all others, some are good and some are bad.

Tada Chimako seems completely free of the crude notion that a poet should be simply the conduit for a flow of energy (e/motion) that starts out there somewhere in "perfect" nature. The highly cultivated and intelligent translator of Marguerite Yourcenar, Claude Levi-Strauss, and the Nobel poet Saint-John Perse could hardly be injured by the term "intellectual poet." She is one; a very good one—who's work promises to bring some freshness of language and thought into a contemporary Japanese poetry that too long has tended toward excessive sentimentality about both life and writing.

Tada in her essay "The Mirror of Velasquez" says that "In poetry all the elements work functionally, each word having a numerical value that changes constantly along with the changes of syntax. When dealing with even a short poem the reader must engage his intellectual energy to follow an equation of almost infinite complexity. How does such difficult work come to be experienced as pleasure? Because the concrete images and situations and structures presented by the poem satisfy not only the senses and the emotions but also the brain's capacity for performing intellectually delicate work. And when to that satisfaction with decoding is added the poetic impact of glimpses of the utterly unexpected, of some other world, the resulting pleasure can approach that bliss which is among the most sublime experiences available to humans."

This reflection on reading is also an assertion of principles at work in Tada's writing of poetry. She says quite clearly that intellect, feeling, and the senses can combine to create the most sublime pleasure, bliss, that a most intellectual poet can also be most sensual. "Me," one of her earliest poems, already sings this discovery of the union of intelligence and sensuality.

Me

Happy as a cabbage
I am planted in the earth.
When I carefully strip away the words
I'm wearing
my absence is revealed—
and the existence of my roots.

Tada uses the title "Me" here to present not just one more example of Romantic self-expression; the poem atomizes, de-individualizes, the so-called "self" in order to resolve it to elements of a universal substance. And so she reveals that her idea of poetry is not so far from that of the Greek poet who said that "a person is a dream dreamed by a shadow." Also revealed is her commitment to the Buddhist idea of Nirvana. This joining of Hellenism and contemplative Buddhism is characteristic of Tada's poems; it is one result of her ongoing concern to eliminate egocentrism from her work. Some lines from a much longer poem will help make this clear.

"Universe of the Rose" records a visionary experience Tada had while contemplating a rose for several hours during an experiment with LSD in 1963.

            . . . one rose—universe rotating round the
                    ever opening center of a flower
        wriggling out of dense red darkness
        sevenfold eightfold petals evolving
                    toward gossamer rarity

        then abruptly from the depths of the rose
        a whirlwind rises
        words that like a calyx had covered the flower
        unable to endure any more   burst
        bend backward and weep . . .

What is continuously expanding here is the Rose Vision, but what strikes Tada most profoundly is the appearance of "words that like a calyx had covered the flower/unable to endure any more   burst/bend backward and weep. . . ." What then are these dynamic petals of a continuously whirling rose, petals that spring outward like a whirlwind? They are the active state of the *signifié* in poetic creation, a *signifié* that constantly overflows to break through the enveloping *significant*, the actual words.

            . . . what kind of existence could be a balance
            at the center of this ever-expanding rose universe
            (place a polished bronze mirror
            before the pollen-covered soul). . . .

Tada, in the thrall of her Rose Vision, has experienced the everlasting explosion of supra-rational elements that lies at the very center of poetic creation. And, paradoxically, this "intellectual poet" deserves that title precisely because of her deep, even sensual sensitivity to this ever-coming-into-being world that surpasses intellect itself—it is at this juncture that her metaphysics becomes unified with her poetic praxis.

Tada Chimako is the first Japanese woman poet to establish her own poetic world in this manner. Through a tireless exploration of the fundamental principles of poetic creation she has come to occupy a unique position in Japanese poetry.

Tada Chimako
The Poems

Dead Sun

shedding beads of light
the child crawls up
into a world not yet wrinkled

turns a somersault
the hourglass flips
a new time begins

the child picks up stars to skip like stones
ancient fish laugh and flip their fins
splashing the feet of god

soon the child grows
heavy with memories
the world is filled with footprints

yawning
the child leaves
dead sun stuck in his pocket.

Me

Happy as a cabbage
I am planted in the earth.
When I carefully strip away the words
I'm wearing
my absence is revealed—
and the existence of my roots.

Wind Invites Wind

wind invites wind
to devour the wolf
blue flesh   quick blood
oh cedar of night   tower of the night

the pollen irresistably swells and falls
and the moon rounds a white eye
let wind eat wind
let bone bite bone

the breathing gropes and the monkeys cower
piling one fossilized cry on another
oh cedar of night   tower of the night
a glass bird shatters into splinters

rails pierce the forest
red cracks the oven
again wind invites wind
to devour the wolf

A Poetry Calendar

I who wait for myself
I who don't appear
again today I turn a page of the sea
throw away a tight-lipped dead clam

    the day   not quite dawn   the beach white
    a mother's barren womb   a broken oar

I who wait for myself
I who don't appear
again today I turn a page of the horizon
throw away a snake's too light slough

    the day   not quite dawn   a useless parasol
    a suspicious laugh   cold fried food

I who wait for myself
I who don't appear
again today I turn a page of the sky
sweep together and throw away all the sooty stardust

    the day   not quite dawn   the grass full of hanging tears
    I leaf and leaf through a calendar
    yet I don't appear
    I who wait for myself
    world of imaginary numbers   love without arms

Song

I'll not carve anything in stone
I won't scrape up sand or mud
I've already come to where I am
Why would I not leave

there is the desert
there are the sun and the distances
I've come here
straight
like wind filling a void

I who was once the sea
will not seek the buried bones, or the veins of white water
in the shade of sand dunes that repeat questions and answers
I'll not seek worn triangular sails or dirty tents
sailing through dry waves
neither will I be tempted by the swift swirling tornado
that rope ladder to the sky

there is the desert
there are the sun and the denials
I've come here
straight
along the road ruled by yesterday

time is always asking questions about form
space answers only with matter
trailing a black shadow that blesses me from behind
I've already come to where I am
why would I not leave

King's Army

on the mountain beyond plains lives a goddess
she it is who hangs up storm clouds
like a scarf she's done waving at a lover

with a large army
the king advances towards sun's dinner table
a touch of cold makes the old general sneeze
and each time he shoots out a loose tooth
thus does he move planting his teeth in the road

(from those scattered teeth tiny men sprout
again and again only to be trampled by the ranks of troops)

—eyes unable to see the visible will see the invisible
        oh prophet
your blind eye   what coming calamity does it reflect?

—laughter in heaven
inundation on earth

a huge lump of rock salt crushing the chosen slave's back
little by little dissolves in sweat
flows and in a moment dries
three days later
he becomes a pillar of shining salt

(salt pillars raised every three miles—
glory of the ever advancing king)

*

various kinds of actions of various kinds of men
he who as an offering to the goddess on the mountain
carries his own head in a leather bag
he who repeats
suzukake no ki ni suzugata no tamashii ga suzunari ni natte
kazee fuku tabi ni suzuyaka ni natte ita[1]
(the liar's tongue has been pulled out)
he who digs a hole deeper than the well
puts a candle on his head and

tries to descend to the lower world
or the man pondering ways to fall
to the bottom of zenith's funnel
he who day in day out holds a thermometer to his temple
to check the temperature appropriate to reason
all are noted in the margin of the chronicle

incidentally the nude coffee-colored boys are
graceful linear letters dancing in the desert
(deciphering them is the old general's secret pleasure)

*

the war is always at the far end of earth
and the only kind of information brought
is that one after another pomegranates burst
on the sun's dinner table

no end to this line of battle
camping on the river bank
horses and camels drinking so
the river dries up

an army so huge
no one knows where the commander-king is
a little girl who comes to offer him a warm goose egg in a silk slipper
is lost
in the labyrinth of the soldier's eyes

an army so huge
while pushing from century to century
someday finally will interrupt Time

a sorceress by the river
watching stones grow and multiply
(like moss on a stone
a beard grows on her chin)

*

hidden in the beehive pod of the emptied lotus
the larvae the helpless spectors await their time to emerge

evening sun about to ignite
the unexploded thunder held quiet in the stony mountain

at that moment around a column of purple cloud
hovers and spirals toward heaven a giant phantom butterfly

seen by a camel squatting apart
or by the grainy granular ticks
stuck to the rims of its eyes
(of course the man picking picking ticks as if counting rosary beads
had his back turned to the sky)

The Odyssey or "On Absence"

1

You, Odysseus trainer of the wooden horse of pleasure
you made your wife swoon in ecstasy with the ardor of your breath
when the shadowy warriors jumped
every night from the broken sides of the wooden horse
Troy burned in the name of Penelope

You who started home a long time ago
wearing around your neck ornaments of the dead gods killed by fire
you were always on the waves
always in the shade of rocks
Did that seashell dissolve
in the clear acid sea
and the bittersweet pearl in the shell too
Is Ithaca still swaying on your brow
like a distant star
Is the small island still on your tongue
surrounded by bubbles
not dissolved in the sour saliva
on your broad warm tongue

2

The son grew up perched on the tallest treetop on the island
looking out over the open sea
Every ship could be the Royal one bearing his absent father
the god who did not even have to exist in order to rule

In an angelic moment
Telemachus flew through the sky
alighting on the mast of a ship on the sea
Oh how much like his thoughtful father
the rising grey head of the cresting wave
The mast abruptly tilts
like a scale that has lost its balance

When someday Odysseus returns
his son will for the first time doubt his father's presence
He will fall like a live bird with its wings torn off

But now
by the flowing current bringing along the seasons
by all the silver fish living in the sea
every ship could be that Royal one bearing his absent father

3

In the lonely womb—the warm water clock—
your wife crushes grapes one by one
trickling the juice into the empty space
thereby she is gradually relieved of weight
During the long years of absence
the clusters of grapes have all been crushed
and Penelope is no longer even a woman

In her hands worn out in the act of waiting
the thread will snap one day
the spindle that has been turning will stop
and you will appear out of the shade of the rocks
a man who is husband father and king
white hair streaming over your face like the crest of a breaking wave

The suitors will recede muttering like an ebb tide
With doubtful wondering eyes she will look at you

from silence as wide and white as her sandy beach
in sunlight as thick as swarming flies
at Odysseus no longer the hero of the tale

4

The slaughter is finished   Let us have music
The uninvited are all murdered in the course of the banquet
by another uninvited guest

Stepping over the slain bodies
you call the musicians   Let us have music
(All this while Penelope sleeps)

The feast must go on
Lukewarm blood is poured into the wine jar
Let the water and sponge cleanse the foul remembrance
while Penelope sleeps
And oh for some music
oh for a flute to comb her hair
oh for a harp to relax her cheeks
after the ceremony of murder
Closing her eyes to all this
Penelope sleeps on
reluctant to wake from a twenty year dream

Universe of the Rose

lysergic acid diethylamide

Each of these microscopic points and lines is in itself a complete world;
so size and density exist there in precisely inverse proportion.[2]

Prologue

one rose—
here is the whole range of crimson tones
this sweep of colored petals is a chain of being
joining sky to earth, future to past
I go down the scale, glissando
glimpse the compound eyed prime mover
concealed in folds of flower petals still unborn
immortal spider weaving its web toward infinity. . . .

Universe of the rose

one rose—universe rotating round the ever opening center of a flower
wriggling out of dense red darkness
sevenfold eightfold petals evolving toward gossamer rarity

then abruptly from the depths of the rose
a whirlwind rises
words that like a calyx had covered the flower
unable to endure any more   burst

bend backward and weep
(bloodshot compound eyes of the petals!)
the intestines of the rose are a coiled snake
glittering scales in bloom
odor of smouldering pollen
(sunspots multiply)

the countless dead buried in the flower core
in orderly piles spread like a fan
slowly regain their color and one by one stand

out of obscure folds in the undulating waves
simultaneously surges a multitude of coral insects
climbing the flesh-colored atoll

what kind of existence could be a balance
at the center of this ever-expanding rose universe
(place a polished bronze mirror
before the pollen-covered soul)

this flower born from me continually giving birth to me
when stepping on the color tones I follow the spiral staircase
innumerable butterflies rise from the dense grass of my hair
my eyes are dazzled by fragrance
then the spider
huge spider with radially extended legs hangs over me

oh whirlwind   overturning all the ships
funnel sucking them down the purple abyss
slowly rotating
aimed at a shoal of fish in the air
the cast net swiftly spreads

in consummate darkness
the rose had shaken off its withered words
on Libra the Balance
tilted strongly toward daybreak it stood
and roared   all its petals trembling

Epilogue

the universe is the work of an instant
as are all dreams
the divine dream also is short
infinity like rose nectar is hidden in this moment

even in the recreating of daily life
every fragment is given endless shades of color
the dream again and again survives the explosions
my bones will be adorned with the rose

Lost Kingdom

one tradition has it that in reality there were no kingdoms
yet only the royal pedigrees last
like veins in dead leaves

memory is severed
memory's roots are cut off
must we descend into the Land of Roots[3]

*

close the eyes   become citizen of darkness
sleep will slip through into the depths
from Cretaceous to Jura
from Devonian to Cambrian
continually falling like the white whiskers of an old Taoist hermit

(in the underground currents of the Land of Roots
the gods of shadow must throng)

*

time at each moment possesses boundless space
vast desert studded with countless kingdoms
the king of one moment's small kingdom is me
look at the always humid hollow of my palm —

this boundless space is there
to reveal the Line of Fate crossing it

*

in the desert a wheel rolls
rolls and grows bigger
brightness of its radiating spokes
deafening grind of the sun wheel!
let me ask   is anyone born to this world
who has not suffered the punishment of the wheel

(suppose a great tortoise shell were turned over
the soft flesh and ovaries exposed to day
suppose this is done solely as a favor to the hyena)

*

at evening the water jar of heaven is gently tilted
and the stars flow out
(the question the answer circling the celestial sphere of my skull
two satellites that will never meet)

from dune to dune are scrolled
one after the other the esoteric writings—
at least spell out the cuneiform of lightning
the purple cipher smelling of fires to come

the spear I throw at the horizon
infallibly will pierce me in the back
from my wound
out will creep a wriggling snake
along the meandering crimson Euphrates
kings with curly bronze beards

draw nearer on sphinx-back
(meanwhile on the big sandstone wall
fervently growing arabesques
neither color nor thickness only intertwined lines
allow not even an amoeba's existence)

*

people barely settled in illusory towers
who talk eat sleep in mirages
must some day fall from their castles in the air
but the young man there stooping gracefully
to tie the lace of his gold sandal
to him life so far is solid architecture
death no more than a legend

*

give dreams to the dead
reverse the tide   turn desert into sea
all kingdoms sink into the Land of Roots
this is the beginning of everything
the soul suspended in midair
looks down at the drowned history
and I a small king of a small kingdom that was lost—
in the crown of my head is a hole
into which each time a kalpa[4] passes
a falling petal drops

Jungle Gym
from *The Territory of Children*

This world is made up of angles only, indicating many cubes.

But the geometrical abstraction is somewhat reduced by the width and weight of iron bars.

Segments of a certain length, keeping a rectangular contact with other segments, proliferated upward and downward, toward north, south, east, and west, to make this world.

According to another tradition this world is the offspring of a square bubble that gradually multiplied and swelled. It has not even so thin a membrane as a bubble.

This transparent world was by no means created to be a cage, but to permit free passage.

Branches arranged at equal intervals allow us to move from one bar to the next without touching the ground. Inhabitants of the jungle gym world have an idea that the existence of the world's frame deserves trust. But here and there the iron bars are removed so cunningly that even monkeys sometimes fall.

Seen straight on it is a fragment of common graph paper. If you shift your glance you will find that behind each square other duplicate squares lie in ambush. A plane figure is folded into a three-dimensional space.

True, these cubes are equivalent to each other, but the difference of their positions sketches out a hierarchy, the social structure of this world. First, there is a difference between upper and lower in the strict sense of the words. Next comes the differences between the outer and the inner.

Those cubes that belong to the lowest class have one of their six facets identified with the ground. Other cubes are members of the highest class, though their desire to rise to heaven is severed at the outset. The rest form an intermediate class between the extremes. The hierarchy composed of all these cubes exists a priori and solemnly.

Cubes in the inner area share four or all six facets with neighboring cubes and so form a perfect community. The outermost cubes expose at least one facet, at most five, to the outside: thrusting their faces against the hollow wind of the outer world. They are in fragile solidarity, eroded by solitude, afraid of the moment when they will be disconnected from the community.

This is the world of plurality. Once a wise grammarian differentiated between quantitive and numeric plurality: the former has as its premise the concept of mass, the latter the concept of division.

Doesn't the jungle-gym world satisfy both simultaneously and perfectly?

It should be regarded as an empty mass capable of division into equivalent spaces.

This structure is a small fragment of a countable set. In spite of its vigorous desire to proliferate infinitely toward high heaven this basic set is bound to earthy finite things by the various human conditions.

I have offered here some ideas about the jungle-gym; ideally these could proliferate infinitely, but they are forced by their own condition to remain within a finite state. I have offered here a basic set of concepts — a small apparatus to play with, offered to a *homo ludens* fed up with walking on the ground.

---

[1]On the platan tree bell-shaped souls grew in abundance; every time the wind blew they rang refreshingly.
[2]Fictional quotation ascribed to Nicolas Cusanus.
[3]A place not unlike Hades.
[4]Sanskrit for a very long time, not eternity.

Ōoka Makoto

Ōoka Makoto

by Miura Masashi

Ōoka Makoto was born in 1931 in Mishima, a city located on a stretch of Pacific shore between Tokyo and Kyoto widely known for its great natural beauty. Both his parents were teachers, and his father, Ōoka Hiroshi, was a noted poet in tanka form and the editor of the tanka magazine *Bodaiju* (Bodhi Tree). The 31-syllable tanka has the longest history of any Japanese poetic form, yet it has managed to adapt itself to the modern world and to develop into a subtle yet dynamic contemporary form. Thus Ōoka Makoto lived with traditional Japanese literature as part of his everyday world while he was young, an experience that continues to influence his poetry at the deepest levels.

Ōoka made his debut, however, not as a poet rooted in ancient Japanese tradition but as a poet coming to terms with the French tradition, from symbolism to surrealism. One of the first poets to practice surrealism in Japan, he was exploring new and important territory. After graduating from Tokyo University, he first gained prominence when he published his *Essay on Éluard* in 1952, when he was thirty-one. Although this was a fortunate event for Japanese poetry, it was not equally fortunate for Ōoka himself. He published his first poems—including "For Spring"—at the same time as his essay, but it soon became difficult for him to go beyond his image as an outstanding essayist and critic. Thus the publication of his first book of criticism, *Essays on Modern Poetry* (1955), preceded that of his first book of poems, *Memory and Presence* (1956).

In 1954 Ōoka joined a group of poets that included Kawasaki Hiroshi, Ibaragi Noriko, and Tanikawa Shuntarō, who put out the magazine *Kai* (Oar). The Oar group marked a departure from the poems of the older Wasteland group, which was made up of survivors of the disaster of World War Two. Ōoka soon emerged as the theoretical leader of the new Oar group, and during the 1950s and early 60s his literary criticism tended to overshadow his equally outstanding poetry. His essays covered the full range of contemporary arts and had a decisive influence on modern Japanese intellectual life. Like the other surrealists, Ōoka left no area or art unexamined. His widely-read critical works include: *Art Minus 1* (1960), *Critique of Lyricism* (1961), *Art and Tradition* (1963), *Eyes, Words, Europe* (1965). During this period Ōoka became good friends with the songwriter Takemitsu Tōru and the painter Kanō Mitsuo.

In 1959 the magazine *Alligator* began to appear. It carried the poems of Ōoka, Yoshioka Minoru, Kiyooka Takayuki, Iijima Kōichi, Iwata Hiroshi, and a number of others, all poets with definite views to express. Even among them, however, Ōoka quickly became the dominant theoretician, playing a role similar to that played by Ayukawa Nobuo in the Wasteland group.

Ōoka's brilliant critical career tended to divert attention from his steady growth as a poet. Ōoka was strongly attracted to surrealism precisely because of his profound, innate understanding of traditional Japanese poetry; he took his painstaking theoretical journeys because of his strong attachment to the world of the senses. In the late 1960s it became clear that the theoretical critic Ōoka was only part of the sensitive, sensual poet Ōoka.

1971 was an important year for Ōoka. His long prose poem, "Her Fragrant Body," was published, along with *Ki no Tsurayuki*, a book about a great tenth-century poet, and *The Emergence of Language*, a collection of essays. The next year *A Perspective—for Summer*, which included "Her Fragrant Body," appeared, and *Ki no Tsurayuki* won the Yomiuri Prize for Literature. After *Memory and Presence* Ōoka had published only one other book of poems, *My Poems and Realities*, in 1962. Then, in 1968, some unpublished works were brought together in *Ōoka Makoto: Collected Poems*. This relatively slim output made Ōoka's post-1971 production all the more spectacular. The *Collected Poems* was a summing up of his earlier period; in *A Perspective—for Summer*, and later books, Ōoka's poems enter new terrain.

The three works published in 1971 showed that within the space called "Ōoka Makoto" there had taken place an important meeting and union of traditional and modern Japanese poetry. This was surely inevitable from the start; yet, also inevitably, it took almost two decades to accomplish. It took that long for Ōoka to find a way to embody concretely his notion that, far from the poet expressing her- or himself with words, it is words which express themselves with and through the poet. He further demonstrated that women play a crucial role in this process—at least in as far as this process embodied and involved him. For Ōoka, women are another name for imagination itself. For him it is not the poet who imagines; it is imagination which seduces the poet. Images of women play the all-important intermediary role.

"Her Fragrant Body" is this notion become poem; *The Emergence of Words* is the translation of this concept into poetry; and *Ki no Tsurayuki* is a demonstration, using classical tanka poetry, of how this notion is required by the nature of verbal art itself. Tsurayuki, the compiler of the *Kokinshū* (Ancient and Modern Collection; completed around 905), the first imperial poetry anthology, and a tanka poet of equal stature with Fujiwara no Teika, the poet and co-editor of the *Shinkokinshū* (New Ancient and Modern Collection; 1206) anthology, in many ways represents traditional court poetry itself.

Philosophical concepts, of course, do not appear suddenly or out of nowhere. The environment of classical poetry and learning that surrounded Ōoka when he was young was doubtless important in the formation of his thought, yet this central concept runs, often invisibly, through all of Ōoka's poems, essays, and criticism. As early as 1961, for example, he was writing this about the works of the medieval Sōtō Zen master Dōgen: "Here there exists an absolute universe of expression in which words do not express things; rather, things express themselves as words."

A poet who takes this notion as seriously as it deserves to be taken must above all else commit her- or himself completely to words. And Ōoka, interestingly, has always, from the very start, been a poet giving and committing himself to something. For example, "Fluting on the River Bottom," Ōoka's first important poem (written when he was eighteen) begins:

> Play your flute lightly, on and on
> blow it till your lips turn blue
> sitting on riverbed sand softly scattering
> in the still water only long grass sways

In giving himself to water Ōoka is giving himself to imagination—and to words. It is above all the intensity of Ōoka's commitment that marks him as unique. Consider this passage from "Her Fragrant Body":

> As she held me, as I flew higher, I heard what she was saying. Her breast spread
> out into the distance. Suddenly, dizzy with jealously, I screamed.

The poet who once gave himself to water now abandons himself to a woman's vast breast. In Ōoka's poems words and water and women flow through and around each other to form a single stream. They are the ways in which the cosmos reveals itself. Ōoka's great originality has lain in his ability to raise separate and individual qualities and images to a level at which they fuse organically and form a universal philosophy of language. In this way Ōoka has developed an approach that allows him to move freely back and forth between classical Japanese literature and his own contemporaries. The classics are not at all conservative for him. Poets of the past — Tsurayuki, Teika, Bashō — are as experimental as anyone in the modern age because they continue, timelessly, to give themselves to words, to let language express itself through them. In Ōoka surrealism has come this far.

A Perspective—for Summer was followed by *Below the Tossing and Turning Planets* (1975), *Elegies and Blessings* (1976), *For a Girl in Spring* (1976), and *Water Region: Invisible Towns* (1981). Each is filled with new discoveries, and each newly explored world is more fertile than the last. Since 1979 Ōoka has written so many poems that he has clearly moved from his "theoretical period" into his "poem period."

In 1979 Ōoka began writing a series of daily articles for the *Asahi* newspaper called *Oriori no Uta* ("Songs Sometimes" or "Occasional Songs") that introduced and interpreted outstanding Japanese songs and poems of all ages — from the most anciently recorded times until our own. For this series Ōoka received the Kikuchi Kan Prize. Ōoka's synthetic, editorial talents served, however, not only to raise the level of poetic understanding and sensitivity of the Japanese public but also to confirm and extend his philosophy of language. In this long, almost sinuously flowing series of articles Ōoka, who has recently led a revival of traditional Japanese renga and renku linked verse by writing verses collectively with a number of contemporary authors (one of them the American Thomas Fitzsimmons), was able to editorially link together songs and poems from different ages and forms, thus showing how they are all linked together within a single extended work, the ever ancient yet ever new Japanese poetic tradition.

Ōoka Makoto
The Poems

For Spring

You dig up the sleepy sandy Spring
put it in your hair and laugh—foam
of laughter rippling the air while
quietly the sea warms the green sun.

Your hand in mine, your stone flung
into my sky, shadows of petals deep
overhead: buds shoot out of our arms;
from the center of our seeing shines
the gold-splashing circling sun.

We are the lake, the trees, the sun
filtering down to lawn through branches
to dance on the terraces of your hair.

In the fresh wind a door swings open,
a hand beckons us and the green shadows;
roads on the earth's soft skin are
fresh, and your arms shine in water.

Under the lashes of our eyes,
beneath the sun, fruit
and the sea ripen slowly.

Portrait

Fields & cities sink
into the fresh planes of your brow.

Always you come
from behind   wakening
like a circling offshore breeze;
                    continuity
                        without beginning,
trembling in a wood
where trees have disappeared,
                    eternal noon
                    eternal legend.

Evenings
when flames frame the toes of birds
you are a small fiery cloud;

inside you
                    above your center
                    your high atoll
bright blue fish swim in schools
                    among algae   &
an eye
stares at some distant tower;
                    flamecentered eye.

You are an unsilvered mirror;

I fall into you endlessly;
sometimes I am a swing inside you
                no children around
Autumn sitting quietly upon me.

But mostly you are
                beautiful,
a storm raging back to heaven,
ten fingers stretching
to the edge of the universe
                beyond lightning
                beyond expectation,
fingertips hot & sensitive as lips.

A far breeze
brings the sea back to you—
                sunwarmed &
                excited
you walk forever:

silently proving
                form
                perfect only in motion.

The Colonel and I

Written in the early 1960's as the Korean War came to an end but other wars, as in Algeria, continued, and the production of nuclear weapons increased; dedicated to all Nuclear War Strategists.

Colonel my Colonel
It is I who loves you.
Where are you going at 8 in the morning
School?
Colonel my Colonel
Love you because I love bombs
Big bombs and all
Possibilities rammed
Full and precise
Behind triggers.
Love
All earthquakingly beautiful parts
Shattering together.
And you like a bomb
Colonel my Colonel.

How beautiful the cloud.
Violent vertical leap to thinner air
Wonderful cloud
Blink
Seismometer
Break
Blink
Humanity
Break
Blink
O bird
Break

Colonel my Colonel
From dugout to schoolroom
Precise are your footsteps
And I love them.
Your lectures put Descartes to shame
Should be transcribed into Latin leaflets
Engraved in Kunic and placed on altars
Sanskrit versions pressed to breasts
When death comes
Under the linden tree.
And let him hear let him hear
He who before Columbus
Discovered America.

Colonel my Colonel
Why make bombs?
Why everybody knows bombs
Are made to be dropped
Disposed of
For peace.
Always short of bombs
Because always short of peace
We must make bombs
Whistle whistle whistle whistle.

Colonel my Colonel
When I held your daughter
Close in a rented room
Was it only to dispose of her
Only for that?
Colonel my Colonel

It is I who loves you
Love you because I love bombs
And you are a bomb
And must be disposed of
Dropped
Into Sanskrit poems
Into my own poems
That is an order.

Words/Words

1.

I keep
on a vacant lot
an invisible horse,
ride off sometimes to see
a 12th century Zen priest —
after 800 years
his body's gone,
turned into words,
soon now the words will be gone
"temporary abode til then"
he says
"eaves of words"
he says
& when he says
"flowers open and the world blooms"
it's he who comes open,
he who is the world blooming
as words
within words,
with words
he is opened & closed
floats   sinks
is born   is killed,
continues as words
continues to live in words
cannot die
as long as there are words on earth
he changes

into rocks   wheels   love affairs
blood   sky   calendars,
changing
knowing (hurting) he equals the world.
there's nothing like
the pain
of word turned flesh,
those who do not feel
that pain
he says
have lost touch
with the body
he says,
withered
old
sage.

2.

everyone was using hard words
& I knew that unless I turned parrot
I couldn't charm
wouldn't please
so I went to bed
but all these lips
came to visit
and complain
"dirty words"
"dirty words"
"our ears burn with your words"
"that's silly"
I say   & get up:
"we'll compare your words & mine
& then we'll build Rome
all the Romes;"
& sat
& looked all over my desk
for words,
no words,

not in the room
not in the street
not in the picture frames,
no words
in the wires
in my mouth
in my fingers,
everybody
turned to stone.

I stood stoned
long
a long time,
seasons passed
wind blew on,
seed packed into my pores
rain filled all the hollows
& sand filmed upon me
thin as nothing;
the sun shone
the land changed
the cities changed
I stood still
till finally sound
happened around me,
blossoming
swelling
into wind-storm howl
seedcrack
rainbullets
sandhammers
on a coffin,
even the sun was loud.
I stood still
in seas of silence
till the high sound
happened,
the high
pitched heartbeats

of sound plankton:
"look   hey   these
are the words
the words of nature
these"
I yelled
& yelled
& looked around
& no one there
no people,
constellations
floating in my room,
sound burning in the wood,
ecstasy.
I floated high
drawn by deep
a dark river,
peering
seeing
in the waves way down
a mountain of paper
a universe of words
slowly sinking
settling slowly
for e v e r.

When First You Saw Your Body

When first you saw
your body's
beauty,
like a new word
rolling off the tongue

the flies of the port
still swarmed
on the mackerel
& your sisters slept on,
still dreaming in the shelter
of your father.

The first time you saw
your body's
beauty,
juices held
five hundred years
in your cells
flowed free and

a thousand year old code
opened your flesh
to the void
at the center of creation.

Even a lullaby can offer
the premonition of some
fearful leap.

But your sisters slept on,
still dreaming
in the shelter of your father.

On the horizon
a clown appeared
slowly churning his stick
in a small
moss-covered opening;

contented he sang
low & clear
a song you could not help
but hear
even though you stopped your ears:

"The Other World is full.
This World is full.
Full world breeds full world.

"Take a full world from
a full world and the world's
still full. The thousand
thousand worlds: an empty dream.
Slippery sap. Slippery sap."

Even a lullaby like that
can prefigure some
fearful leap,
when you stare at your body
knowing its beauty.

You became woman,
became orphan,
staring through all your organs
at the small voice
of a flower
opening.

My love,
the trembling of your body
traced
in the shape
of the flower's faint voice

a form found only in flesh
already caught
in Creation's great voice.

The Power in a Starry Sky

For Iijima Kōichi, poet, friend; although this is a love poem, we share some memory of these events.

One Autumn day in my forty-fourth year I
wander a white lime path on Shiranui shore.

Love, do you always tighten your eyes so
against the brightness?

Hooded cranes from the marshes of Manchuria
call out over these Arasaki fields, dark

cranes filling the sky with their cries while
we linger on a beach melting into sunset.

Soon night will curve into a gigantic chair,
and all the night long, acknowledging each other,
blossoms will fall, fruit will slowly grow.

Settling deep into night's great chair we will
stare into the small radiance of our bodies;

and a voice will say, "Of the four sacred
tongues, man knows only the last and least."

And another voice: "Even in a play so quiet
as 'Uncle Vanya' there is a pistol shot."

And there are unspoken words, word unheard, uncomprehended, that can make men kill themselves.

So let's you and I hold each other and stay
awhile on this shore; we'll still find the cliff
at the end of words, at the edge of night.

"I'm drunk and want to sleep. Leave me, friend;
come back, if you like, with your Koto tomorrow." —

so speak my dead Grandfathers, and your
stream, full of fleet sweetfish, wanders,
laughing softly, on.

Three-fourths of the sacred tongues still lie hidden
inside you: rich flicker beneath stone honey, under
fire rain.

But as I go alone into night's deep places,
stepping over the soft crust of your soil,

a fountain smelling of printer's ink, all
of its own, writes Morning! and spider-webs
become songs that stretch to the moon.

And now come two Taoist clowns flying calmly
on wind caught in the skirts of soiled robes;

don't you, listening, hear them laughing: "Oh
those two women see through us so easily!"

Perseverance of reptiles endlessly walking;
irrepressible surge of rising tides:

these will I celebrate as I grieve on your
land: drained, shrunken, shriveled.

My love, since you are always transparent,

inside you I meet everything but you;

nowhere do I find you; you are at once clear
heaven and the earth on this shore. And
the evening sun gathered into newborn buds.

And that cry of the willow dipping its branches
into clear flowing water, isn't that you?

Rising to heaven, earthly celebrations become
a small new radiance; from the end of this white
lime path, melodies rise to sing the starry night.

My love, as we hold each other in
night's great chair, we draw ourselves
and the night closer to

the power in a starry sky.

The Slope of That Hill

For my wife; about our early years together.

See how the slope of that hill seems to shimmer?
It's simply that the leaves turn and tremble together.

Your eyes
                    love
spoke
the black void
of unbeing
at earth's & heaven's beginning.

Through wilderness
we rolled
into future
by a single stone fortress
recalling
its past.

And though the world continued
too hostile
to thaw
the freeze in our smiles

your eyes
                    still
spoke
the black void

of unbeing
at earth's & heaven's beginning.

No sooner free of your lips
your voice soared
to join
wind
and the birds.

In a fire of need,
under flapping pawnshop banners,
we created our ways,
invented our nights;

created a game
of giving
not giving,
                    of roaring
and being amazed.

Afternoons
when silks turned
into tired old clothes,
we fashioned some proverbs
came up with some laughs;

made up a game
of weaving
& woven,
confiding &
                    hiding.

Clear over echoes
of Go stones
                    sounding
on some Hermit's game board,
I let fly in joy

the winged sap of my body.

and again
                    love
your eyes
spoke
the black void
of unbeing
at earth's & heaven's beginning.

Covered in pollen
my ego's stallion changed
& changed,
and each time I looked back
from the corner
your face turned into
a strange thickening forest.

To more subtly shadow
the ripe thoughts
of your nakedness I
mixed into your hair
dew
of brimming heaven

but you continued to shine—
a new celestial body
another liquid
undimmed by the meaning
of even your own speaking.

My love
                    we created
on night's horizon
a play of drumbeats &
undulations,
a game of biting &
                    shyly inviting;

created ourselves
                    guarding
the lean words
we had scratched in the sand.

Man become heavenly fort
for a time shelters woman.
Woman become heavenly fortress
for a time shelters man.

Through wilderness
we rolled
into future
by a single stone fortress
recalling its past.

Now come brief moments,
colored by sorrows
that can't be explained,
graced
                    by sea beats of joy.

See how the slope of that hill seems to shimmer?
It's simply that the leaves turn and tremble together.

A Woman I Often Dream Of

Dragged to the scaffold the woman
to be executed arches back and
from the shadows of her brow casts
spells upon the plaza.

Sighs of the dead ascend through
cracks in the stone scaffold stair.
Restraining a scream a small oleander
sways once, tightens, swallows a sparrow.

The watching crowd is one single
eye fixed on the solitary woman. In
the beauty of one about to die she
lays her spell upon them all.

Soundlessly her heart sucks in the walls
of scorn, fear, murderous desire these
persons have raised against her.

Finally she and they are one.
The sun's heat melts sweetly, curls
lewdly inside each knowing center.

I lick her feet with my eyes,
embrace her eternally in the plaza;
her hair is sucked up toward the sky,
her pale toes open to approaching death.

The killing takes an eternity

to begin; the woman stands, womb
vibrant, drenched in last sweat.

In this hushed spell, this ecstasy,
what will die here is the plaza,
the persons gathered here,

the comfort-flowing fountain,
this poised peacefulness.

For a Girl in Springtime

Hear the mountains,
bellies full of fire,
roar their joy
beat a million drums
as men go pale and run for shelter;

remember:
the same power that lifts you
to the Spring-tide of your living
drives the flooding Autumn rivers
bursts the dams of men;

the same force that lets
eggs of the lion-ant and longhorned beetle
sleep deep in the earth until Spring
drives Autumn's fruit up, up and out
thru the slender veins of trees.

In some western capital I saw
a great many fountains and,
dim under domes, images
adorned with sacred names:

after the long nights of blood
massacre, persecution,
the saints had become as one
massively silent bell,

and still the walls are hung with paintings,
relics of consecrated pain,
as if to teach how the Great
without pain
become small.

My life's neither plain nor honest enough
for martyrdom,
over and over that thought twists
through the winter in my belly,

and if some warlover roared his rage,
fires in his belly,
and shot up a flaming cloud or two
I'd probably go pale.

Yet never forget:
the same power that swells Autumn's
rivers and breaks men's dams
lifts you
to the Spring-tide of your life.

Water Region

To reach the bottom there is only
the ladder of the falls. There are no stairs.
If, in the dry season, when the water's low,
if, at noon, the sky has risen
high beyond blue, go out then
to Maple Leaf Heights, where the suicides go.
If you aren't yet ready for suicide
then, unfortunately, your vision is still bad.
But surely you'll be able to make out
the forest swaying dimly in the depths,
down in the pool below the falls.

But your ears, no matter how good they are,
they'll never hear the words from the pool.
So whether you believe all this or not
depends, yes, on the size of your soul.
Listen.

"When living things wake limbed by peaks and rivers,
not one of these waters and mountains is the same.
Some think water is clear, bright crystals,
yet they cannot drink these jewels as water.
The forest swaying in the pool:
cool towers to the carp and trout
but some souls see ranges of needles
and step back terrified, their hair on end.

> *Yes, it's you.*
> *But that's no reason*
> *to blame yourself.*

"Some think water is a rare flower,
yet they cannot boil and drink a flower.
And some call pure water wildfire.
Others say it is bloody pus.
Still others claim it is emptiness.

> *No, not you, your soul.*
> *But that's no reason*
> *to feel reassured.*
> *Water does more than flow.*

"When living things wake limbed by peaks and rivers,
not one of these waters and mountains is the same.
Faces, arms, legs, each leading elsewhere.
Each eye looks down a different fault of light.

"And if you still believe
that dawn breaks ceaselessly
over people, over every living thing,
the same dawn, simply, surely,
if you believe it, say why,
name the ground you stand on.
Speak!"

The water below the falls
bursts higher and higher
and swallows Maple Leaf Heights.

Ah, but you, you still
stand puffing slowly on your cigarette
on a ledge at noon beneath a cloudless sky
watching a river collide with a mountain
since, luckily, you hear nothing
but the beating of the falls.

Soul Region

They live here
tick-tock, tick-tock, shaking their heads,
back and forth in their rocking chairs
so many, and so many, mothers.

Out in wild seas that took their sons,
farther, farther, where wind veins the waves,
they push with their hips and legs
and move in their rocking chairs: the mothers.

Strips of green and purple seaweed sway
on their calves now brushed by nursing whales
migrating softly in the wake of the sun.
Glowing gelatin light, curtains of the soul.

Cruisers. Battleships. Submarines. Convoys.
Sunk ships gather here
and gaze up at the mothers.
It's the nearest they'll ever come.

Officers and men are boys once more
and play at being waterfilled bodies.
"Oh, how long will you keep this up?
It's dark already, the demons are coming."

Tick-tock, tick-tock, shaking their heads,
rocking their chairs: weeping mothers.
Rain falls, and stops, and falls again.
Intermittent showers, darkly burning, intermittent souls.

Firefly Region

I knew my mother was waiting
in the twilight on the other side

so I was never afraid as I searched
the reed-thick riverbank. (Though I was a coward.)

It's not hard to catch fireflies.
But the smell they make, the riverbed

crawling out through their tiny pores
and turning to dew: "How's my light?

It's the fire of water plants." A smell
you try to get back into when you wake

but in my dreams
its stink made me shudder.

Was my mother really waiting
heavy-breasted in the twilight?

The time she and I caught too many fireflies
and my father yelled down at me like a god—

was she really there that night?
Was my mother really on the far bank?

In daylight, four rivers

wound through the center of the plain

The smell of hot manure and a rapeseed field
shared riddles of the sun with shining skylarks.

High-tension wires whined in the wind,
swayed upward with tangles of kite string.

And only travelers sang the song
about the beauties of the town's old brothels.

One of the rivers broke
behind the school, dropped and disappeared.

In daylight, dace and minnows
swam across each other through the plain.

We caught slugs in the riverbed with glass traps,
but the water in the drop would never stay.

When fireflies light the memory of the scratch
flaring along the girls soft skin as we played doctor

I wander half-awake out toward the far shore
looking for another fire, another smell.

"There's something in your hand, child.
I can tell it's very important.

"Why, your fingertips are all white.
You must be squeezing very hard.

"They're dice, aren't they, white bones.
But they have no eyes. They're just bones."

Was my mother in the twilight
on the other side, was she really there?

200

Renga—Linked Poems

by Ōoka Makoto

Japan's ancient literary tradition put little value on the qualities of abnormal genius, originality, and individuality that made up the romantic notion of the "cursed poet." Rather, the standards for traditional Japanese literature were set by the esthetics of the twenty-one imperial waka poetry anthologies that were compiled by the command of various emperors over a period of more than five hundred years, from the early tenth to the middle fifteenth centuries. This esthetics was predicated on an identification of poetry—in terms of both value and taste—with the refined intellectual and sensuous expressions used at group gatherings called *utage*, a term which can be translated as "poetic feast" or "poetic banquet."

The life rhythms and ways of thinking of the poets belonging to the groups which met at such feasts coincided on many levels. The techniques of the poetic tradition were also communically shared, with great numbers of standard phrases and images being handed down and used unchanged generation after generation. Using old expressions was not a fatal defect for a poet; rather, it was regarded both as a way of saluting and indicating respect for fellow poets who had happened to live in earlier ages and as a clear statement of intention to carry on the tradition. Poems, far from being expressions of individual suffering or uncommon talent, were a form of conversation, often humorous, between members of the feasting group.

Poetry contests and *Renga*, or linked verse, were natural developments in this tradition of conviviality. Renga, in particular, has a long and varied history. It grew from short, simple poetic exchanges in the seventh and eighth centuries to elegant, suggestive works by Sōgi (1421–1502) and other medieval masters and then to the complex, dynamic sequences of haikai linked verse by poets such as Bashō in the late seventeenth century and Buson in the middle of the eighteenth century. Linked verse continues to be written in Japan, and the last decade has seen a significant revival of the form.

It is impossible for me to give a detailed description and analysis of renga here, but it seems necessary to go over a few basic points. The traditional tanka form is made up of thirty-one syllables in five lines. What renga did was to separate the first three lines from the last two, thus creating the first two links of a sequence. Chains of alternating verses of three lines (seventeen syllables) and two lines (fourteen syllables) can continue for various lengths: thirty-six, fifty, a hundred, a thousand, or even ten thousand verses. As a rule, a renga sequence is collectively written by two or more poets, with no two consecutive verses being written by the same poet. The poets must follow a number of complex rules as they write. These rules are more than restrictions, however. They assure continuous change and variability and allow for the inclusion of the chance elements that are part of collective creation.

Subject matter is not fixed. Neither is a special theme pursued throughout every verse. This has been especially true since the time of Bashō and his followers, who, almost three hundred years ago, wrote sequences of thirty-six or a hundred *haikai no renga* — haikai meaning both worldliness and humor — that dynamically and concretely embodied the principle of cosmic, universal change itself. Renga has a multiple-focus structure: it is a collection of associatively linked yet independent verses, each of whose constituent lines also has an independent focus. The person who writes the first verse, therefore, has absolutely no idea where the communal poem is flowing or how it will end. The same, of course, is true for all the participants. The verses that follow are linked only to the immediately preceding verse. Each new verse both interprets the preceding verse and creates a new poetic universe comprised of two verses based on its interpretation, which has given new meaning to the preceding verse. This process continues for as long as the renga sequence goes on. In fact, this process of transformation constitutes one of the greatest challenges — and fascinations — presented by renga. Each transformation is itself transformed; simple linear progression is impossible. Multidimensional relationships arise, allowing the parts and the whole to interact dynamically and organically.

Chance elements play a large part in the writing of this kind of group poem and are essential to a renga sequence. This, however, has resulted in linked verse, which is a form of pure play, being regarded as an outdated method of writing and not worth serious attention by modern Japanese poets and critics, who demand an intimate logical and ethical connection between author and work and who operate with a conscious, rational notion of poetry that gives primary value to self-assertion and self-expression. Masaoka Shiki, who exerted such a major influence on early modern tanka and haiku, regarded traditional renga in just such a light. Thus, for many years after the beginning of westernization, renga was overlooked and abandoned by all but a few scholars, critics, and enthusiasts.

A general reexamination and reevaluation of the meaning of traditional Japanese poetry has taken place in the last twenty years, however, bringing with it renewed interest in one of the most important aspects of premodern poetry, communal poetic creation. The haikai no renga (usually referred to as *renku*) of Bashō and his followers has become the object of sensitive and penetrating new studies that have yielded many fresh insights and discoveries. I myself have tried to explore meanings that collective creation can have in our age by actually participating, with several other poets and novelists, in the writing of a number of renku sequences. I have also written several essays in which I analyze renga as the site of dynamic mutual interaction and conversation between elements of collective creation inherent in the traditional poetic feast and elements which each individual poet brings to the work out of his or her spiritual solitude and aloneness, using as illustration a wide range of classical Japanese poems.

Interestingly, just as this reevaluation of traditional poetry began to gain momentum in Japan, an experiment took place in Paris in which four poets gathered and wrote a collective poem directly inspired by the methods and approach of renga. For five days, from March 30th to April 3rd, 1969, the Mexican, Octavio Paz, the Italian, Eduardo Sanguineti, the Englishman, Charles Tomlinson, and the Frenchman, Jacques Roubaud gathered in a Paris hotel and collectively wrote a collection of poems published under the title *Renga* (Gallimard, 1971). As an approximate European equivalent to the tanka, these poets chose the sonnet, a form usually having four parts (two quatrains and two tercets) and a total of fourteen lines. Some sonnet forms, of course, vary in the number of parts, but all have a total of fourteen lines. Paz and the other poets wrote twenty-seven fourteen-line sonnet-like poems, breaking up each poem into four parts, with each part being written by a different poet. The order of authors was changed from poem to poem, and poem parts ranged in length from two to four lines. Each poet, of course, wrote in his own native language. The poems were written in four sequences, the first three of which have seven poems and the last of which has six. The four sequences are numbered I–IV horizontally and 1–7 vertically, except for sequence IV, which contains only 1–6. While the Japanese renga progresses by means of an alternation of two-line and three-line verses, the sonnet form contains significantly longer internal parts and allows for even more complex links and associations.

If the twenty-seven poems are read as a single long poem, the universe that is revealed is far more chaotic than that found in any Japanese renga sequence. Yet *Renga* was an extremely interesting experiment. What it achieved, I think, was a combination of chance, originality, boredom, and unintelligibility that transcends simple categories like success and failure.

Renga intersects, however, with several problems of crucial importance for modern literature, and for the Japanese too it proved to be a very stimulating and suggestive experiment.

When it was published, *Renga* carried, significantly, a dedication to surrealist André Breton. Surrealists, of course, carried out great numbers of experiments in their attempt to pull down concepts like individuality and originality, which had been enshrined on high altars by romanticism, and to replace them with, above all, inspiration. The magnitude of the influence of these experiments on contemporary poetic and other literary thinking goes without saying. At stake is the overthrow of the self-worshipping notion that what controls a work is the author him- or herself. This was where the poets who participated in the creation of *Renga* discovered contemporary meaning in traditional Japanese renga. Creating poems communally, they saw, means writing in a space fundamentally without individuality or personality.

Octavio Paz, in his essay "The Moving Center," which is included in *Renga* (it is called the "Introduction" in the English-language edition), touches on this point:

> The practice of renga implies the negation of certain cardinal western notions, such as belief in the soul and in the reality of the I. The historic context in which it was born and developed did not know the existence of a creator god and denounced the soul and the I as pernicious illusions. Further, each in its own way, Buddhism, Confucianism, and Shintoism, fought against the idolatry of the I . . . renga must have offered to the Japanese the possibility of going out from themselves, of passing from the anonymity of the isolated individual into the circle of exchange and recognition. Also it was a way of liberating themselves from the weight of hierarchy. Although it was governed by rules as strict as those of etiquette, its object was not to put a brake on spontaneity, but to open up a free space so that the genius of each one could manifest itself without doing harm either to others or to oneself. (*Renga*, N.Y., George Braziller, p. 21)

Paz's conclusions match exactly those I myself have come to after participating in the writing of many renku sequences. Even this short passage reveals how accurately Paz understands renga—and how well he must have transmitted this understanding to the other poets. Paz also confesses, however, to suffering considerable pain during the five days of creation:

> A practice which contradicts the beliefs of the West, the renga was for us a test, a purgatory in miniature. As there was no question of either a tournament or a competition, our natural animosity found itself without employment: neither a goal to be attained nor a prize to be carried off, no rival to be vanquished. A game without adversaries. From the first day, in the basement room of the Hôtel St. Simon and during the following days, from March the thirtieth to April the third, irritation and humiliation of the I . . . (*Renga*, pp. 21–22)

When I first began to write renku with several friends some years ago I experienced feelings almost identical to these described by Paz. I also experienced the "confusion," the "sensation of oppression," the "feeling of shame," the "feeling of voyeurism," and the other unpleasant feelings to which Paz confesses. These feelings made me acutely aware of the fact that, although I was brought up immersed in Japanese tradition, I am also a modern poet and, whether I like it or not, have a Western sense of self-consciousness in the heart of my creative consciousness.

Explaining what he means by "a feeling of shame," Paz writes:

> I write in front of others, the others in front of me. Something like undressing in a cafe, or defecating, crying before strangers. The Japanese invented the renga for the same reasons and in the same manner in which they bathed naked in public. For us, the bathroom and the room in which we write are totally private places, where we come in alone and where we realize acts that are alternately infamous and glorious. (*Renga*, p. 22)

This confession vividly shows just how far the new experience of collective creation dragged the poet from his ordinary sensibility, and it is extremely interesting despite the fact that the Japanese did not actually invent renga in the same way that they strip naked in public bath-houses!

In any case, Paz shows great confidence when he writes:

> Our attempt naturally enters into the tradition of modern western poetry. One could even say that it is a consequence of its dominant tendencies: the conception of writing as a combined act, the narrowing of the frontier between translation and original work, the aspiration toward a collective (and not collectivist) poetry. (*Renga*, p. 24)

This first, experimental Western renga differs from the traditional renga of Japan in many respects, yet it unexpectedly revealed universality within Japan's literary tradition.

In the fall of 1981 the American poet Thomas Fitzsimmons and I made another attempt to write an international renga. Loosening many rules but remaining faithful to the basic renga form, we created a sequence of twenty poems called *Yureru kagami no yoake* in Japanese and *LINKED POEMS: Rocking Mirror Daybreak* in English. The many insights I gained from this experience also match those of Paz.

During the collective creation of a poem or poems, each poet must make a constant effort to dissolve his or her own self-consciousness into the space of the group. On the other hand, however, and this is the most fascinating part, collective creation holds within it a great paradox: the self, which seems to have been sacrificed to the group, actually asserts itself all the more clearly. The very method by which self-consciousness is eliminated ensures that the individuality of each poet inevitably shines forth. In fact, the most important quality required of a poet participating in collective creation is that he or she be extremely individualistic. This is indeed a paradox, yet poetry itself comes into being only through a similar paradox consisting of both individuality and supra-individual words.

Rocking Mirror Daybreak

20 Linked Poems—Ōoka Makoto
and Thomas Fitzsimmons

1   Poetry

sink
don't leap.

be silent:

a string
to wind around

autumn.

Ōoka

2   Autumn

Trees strip to bone
leaving color to the wind;
bare bones against heaven's robe
calling down the deep long
white long songs,
the snows.

The silence.

Fitzsimmons

3 Silence

Pancakes
on the fire.

The balloon hasn't
come yet;
time
to sip one last coffee.

The whole codebook
destroyed.

—Take another pancake.
—There'll be no
more mail.
—I'll be the last one
to hear you
crunching walnuts
in this so-called
Shelter.

Still no balloon
on the horizon.

Ōoka

4 Horizon
   (Thanksgiving Day 1981)

Today we look out
far as we can
from this shelter
of wood stone & glass
to where lake & sky
meet in old friendship:
deep water bowl holding
flowering

sky.

                                    Fitzsimmons

5 Sky

Sky in Japanese is *Sora*:
Void between Earth & Heaven:
the Unfounded, the Groundless,
the falsehood, the lie.
And truly sky is sky because
it is ground-less.

I chatted yesterday in the deep
of sky with a beautiful young
storm singing, boasting of being
the million-fingered destructive
aspect of that God of Creation

Shiva.

Ōoka

6 Shiva

Once in exasperation Lord Shiva turned
us into pigeons. Not all of us;
some. Only some of some of us. We
were already many. Now we are more,
and more exasperating, fluttering
about him like small cooing storms,
and he dances us more slowly
thinly into & out of Form, into & out
of Time.
       Shiva & his sublime golden
Shakti, his beloved other dancing Maker,
dancing us into & out of love.
               A bird,
says my beloved Karen, precedes us,
a green and golden bird
           in the shadows.

Fitzsimmons

7 In the Shadows

"Tension lying between opposite stars
keeps this tree always dancing," says
a woman come from far beyond
Chrysanthemums and November fog.

As if sprung from the sea, now and then
a tree, pregnant with dew, trunk drenched
in dew, swings up its roots, shakes down
multi-colored eggs of birds; but the new dawn
always comes.

That tree must have grown by a creek
in my homeland Pluto: I feel the pulse-
enigma of that planet forcing me to be
its destined opposite.

Before us, that woman and I,
dancing slowly still:

the tree.

                                              Ōoka

8　Tree

Man shaft, hair of woman dancing
in air by water, rough-barked Shaman-
road from demon dark to visionary heaven;
sacred to the Mothers, haven
of the Warrior Gods, Christ's green tent;

lifting into morning dew you scratch
the backs of bears & caribou, feed on
sun, root & suck crystal essence
from dark mud deep under stone,
take in our darkened breath, dance
back our necessary air;

old quiet ones.

Fitzsimmons

9   Old Quiet Ones

Second floor, *Palais de*
Chaillot, Musée de l'Homme,
African Masks: superb passage
to the banquet of souls.
Japanese section rather poor.
One item in the South American section
captivates my eyes: smoked human face,
sacred war trophy of some Indian tribe:
enemy head, cut off, skull
pulled out skillfully
through the mouth;
head baked then, by some special process,
until shrunk to grapefruit size;
to my surprise, no wrinkles.

This head
of a once human being,
eyes closed, face calmer than a doll's
hung on truimphal chest,
ruminates now,
passive as a deep-sea fish,
on Time & Eternity.

Must have been a young warrior.
Looks like some terribly old god,
like a newly born babe.

Ōoka

217

10   Newly Born Babe

so now
here you are,
yolked out
of your egg
& cooled,
hauled
from the soft dark,
raw
into wind & glare,
small,
impaled by greed,
stripped of cover,
all mouth
& eyes,
pure presence
trimmed
to pure form,
smooth
as a skull
without its skin.

Fitzsimmons

11   Without Its Skin

Without its metal skin
a plane cannot endure
air's least resistance;
without water skin, the airy
cherry blossom cannot begin
its long floating journey.

Skin touching lover's skin
tingles like the wind
around a crater just before
eruption: tense, acute,
stretched sensitively thin.

The pleasure skin craves is to
approach that zero thickness where
dark of inner flesh, through
membrane thin as light, melts
into another dark of flesh:
first dim light of dawn on skin.

We are all earth skin:
water-streams carrying
petals of flowers unknown.

Ōoka

12   Petals of Flowers Unknown

Black geese scream winter menace at
two overhead passing slim white swans.
Trees urge caution; my old wound flares.
Floundering in ice I beat my way to
Karen, sleeping beside me warm; I
touch her, fill my hands and heart;
wake to the clear cold northern sun.

Last night she spoke her love for
Tim, her brother, dead; and I could
hear, for love of her, Spring
wind singing in a dawn world where
two small burning children
spun and graced each other's days as
simply as crisp morning air
is graced by
petals of an unknown flower,
feather

     of a passing bird.

Fitzsimmons

13 Passing Bird

Up from the body of
young Prince Yamato Takeru
dying
in the Nobono wilderness,
a great white bird ascends,
and Princesses,
weeping, chanting,
struggle day after day
through mud-thick fields
to follow the great bird;

higher and higher the white
bird flies, returning
to heaven;
further and further
the Princesses wander,
returning to dust.

Often in legend dead
heroes become white birds.

October first: before dawn
I lose my father.
From beside
Lake Commerce, Michigan,
following migrating birds,
I have come to his Tokyo hospital,
only to find him in coma;

six hours later he sighs,
slips away to another world.

Rain pours down from dark
night sky; no bird flies.

And no one knows whether my
father became a white bird,
but I know he returned
to the twilight he witnessed
and made into poetry at 25:

> "Evening glow lights now only
> the back of a white waterbird;
> as lake slips into darkness, light
> lingers as delicately as it can."

The glare of lights he had
known all his life all finally
disappeared, but the delicate band
burnishing the feathers of a lake
bird remained in his poet's mind
as a beacon, a distant

galactic stream . . .

Ōoka

14   Galactic Stream

The ice on my window this morning,
transparent bird, white crystal
flower, drinks the rosy light of dawn,
flows it through galactic streams,
swirls it into tropic coral — even
as it warms, begins to melt itself,
its maker,

      white crystal shaper.

Fitzsimmons

15   Crystal Shaper

Not given to staring
at myself in mirrors,
still I know as I write
I shape each poem off
a particular mirror—
sometimes inverting, I
suppose, left and right.

Don't know really if
that mirror hangs in
or outside me.

My friend dreamed
himself a rock giving
birth to blood-red
crystals; we probed
for hidden meanings;
found nothing.

That same night, asleep,
crystal shaper in my
hand, I polished a rock
with human face until
finally I had cut
out of my own hand one
endlessly bleeding

rocking mirror.

Ōoka

16   Rocking Mirror

In the water of this high lake
I see my face
as in the sea long years ago
rocking among the bodies
of friends, bits and pieces
of bodies of friends, not
friends, who knows, how know
which hand is a friend's when
no arm, shoulder, neck, face
completes the hand? how
know how to look so's not to
bleed into your own brain, scream
the salt, gag the wind, the blood
that streaks your hands the boat
the sea your eyes? how forget
the one face, yours, rocking
on the fire, bobbing in a mirror
of human garbage? flame and oil
face streaked
with memories now held cold
in clear blue water.

Fitzsimmons

17   Clear Blue Water

Summer trip to Switzerland;
in our bellies, sausages
eaten on the Zermatt terrace,
foot of the Matterhorn,
slowly turn into
heat: 1000 calories each.

As we climb up and up
the Furka Pass, my eyes
suddenly are perforated
by a billion particles
of heavenly blue:
across the valley a giant
mountain rampart:
The Glacier.

Swinging up its snow-
crowned sky-blue fist,
that ancient water spirit
shouts:

> "From me
> flows
> what you
> call Time."

Down from that colossal
mass of shining ice
flows the majestic
River Rhône.

Ōoka

18   The Majestic River Rhône

Greeks, Romans, Troubadours, Popes
paused by this river, held some sway,

Sous le pont d'Avignon,
On y danse, on y danse . . .

grew quiet, went away.

Disputed all things thought or known:
god, government, what to do on the 1st of May,

Sous le pont d'Avignon,
On y danse, on y danse . . .

grew quiet, went away.

Save that some learned how to dine
and how to quaff the blood-red wine,

Sous le pont d'Avignon,
On y danse, on y danse.
Sous le pont d'Avignon,
On y danse tout en rond.

grew happy, tried to stay.

But only the river knows how to stay,

head in the clouds, grapes on its shoulders,

Sous le pont d'Avignon,
On y danse, on y danse . . .

robes of green trees around its knees.

Fitzsimmons

19   Around Its Knees

On the Tsientang River near Hangchow Bay, south
of Shanghai, soars a giant, stone, eight-faced
pagoda offering walks 'round its knees to workers,
soldiers, families. Massive old giant mortared by
boiled rice laced with fat and blood; few windows,
and small, open to the sun and wind.

In that dim stone place I thought of Gothic
Cathedrals: the shared worship of an up-soaring
empty center. Japanese pagodas are built around
one sacred thick high pillar, a tree, from
whose widespread arms hang three or five storeys
of many-windowed rooms, roofs extended smoothly
like spread wings of birds coming down to rest:
mirroring the spirit of a Japanese Buddha.

But the stone structures of China, France, Italy,
take the shape of a bird driving up through
storm and rain, wings straining back to the limit
of strength. From such power, such driving will,
perhaps was born the old Chinese golden civilization,
the new Western spaceship ways.

That night in my Hangchow hotel I fell on my bed,
wings spread, and slept deeply as a winter leaf
on the small high branch of some tree deep
in a valley where civilizations meet.

Ōoka

20 A Valley Where Civilizations Meet

It is good to meet in valleys—
out of the wind, by water,
where deer and tiger come to drink
at dawn, at sunset, and all day long
men and women trade, give news, swap
stories, change.

        Such deep places
between high mountains are full of
talk: voices ringing down the streams,
mixing, as the waters mix, the deepest,
oldest claims of place and time,
taming the strange into considered
ways.

    Where words mix, ring in the hunt,
sway in barter, banter, challenge, love—
there is

      poetry.

Fitzsimmons

Tanikawa Shuntarō

Tanikawa Shuntarō

by Miura Masashi

Tanikawa Shuntarō was born in Tokyo in 1931, the only child of the famous philosopher Tanikawa Tetsuzō. He hated school from the start, constantly rebelled against his highschool teachers, and never even considered going to college. Then, in 1950, Miyoshi Tatsuji, an outstanding older poet, recommended Tanikawa's poems to the prestigious literary magazine *Bungakkai*, which printed several of them. Tanikawa had suddenly become a famous poet when only nineteen. Two years later, in 1952, Tanikawa's first book, *Two Billion Light Years of Solitude*, appeared. It marked a clear new direction in postwar Japanese poetry.

The poetry written in the years immediately after Japan's surrender in 1945 was dominated by the Wasteland group. Wasteland poets such as Tamura Ryūichi succeeded in fusing the methods of modernism with the intensity of their wartime experiences, creating a poetics in which life and death stood for each other. Tanikawa presented an alternative vision of the postwar world, a young, innocent vision without the shadow of war and defeat. Tanikawa's poems inspired and showed the way for a whole generation of young poets. In 1953 his second book, *Sixty-Two Sonnets*, came out. This was also the year he joined the Kai (Oar) group, which had recently been started by Kawasaki Hiroshi and Ibaragi Noriko. This group, which was soon joined by Yoshino Hiroshi, Tomotake Shin, Ōoka Makoto, Mizuo Hiroshi, Kishida Eriko, Nakae Toshio, Iijima Kōichi, and others, made a lasting contribution to post-Wasteland Japanese poetry.

As indicated by the title *Two Billion Light Years of Solitude*, Tanikawa Shuntarō's early poems are marked by a unique cosmic sensibility. These poems express

Tanikawa's passage from the self-centered world of youth out into the infinite expanses of the universe itself; and many of them deal with the dizzying moments the young man finds himself on the cliffs of his own borders. In "Museum," for example, a poem included in Tanikawa's first book, the image of a museum suggests the existence of an infinity of time staring in at our present world. The self comes into existence by taking itself for an other and then coming to regard that other as itself. Tanikawa intuitively realized this and went on to see in this dramatic process the origins of the modern age itself. For him, and this is crucial, infinity is a realm of silence—the silence of the museum—and thus silence has the upper hand over language. The following is one stanza of sonnet 30 from *Sixty-two Sonnets*:

> Surrounded by things that don't speak
> only humans talk, talk too much—
> and the sun, trees, clouds
> aren't even aware of their own beauty

Nature is silent; humans are language. In this poem silent nature is seen as fortunate and language-using humanity is clearly unfortunate. Yet Tanikawa realizes that he must go on writing, no matter how unfortunate he may be. This contradiction is the deepest theme running through *Sixty-Two Sonnets*. Thus the last stanza of sonnet 11, a poem subtitled "Silence," goes:

> No more voice, no words
> no muttering, no song, no cough even
> but I—must speak everything

Tanikawa continued to speak in book after book: *On Love* in 1955, *Picture Book* in 1956, *For You* in 1960, *21* in 1962, and *Ninety-Nine Satirical Songs* in 1964. But the contradiction between words and silence continued to force itself on him, hidden behind an impressive number of stylistic experiments, as his central theme. Then, in 1968, Tanikawa's famous collection *Journey* was published. Its opening poem, "Toba 1," begins:

> I have nothing to write
> my body is exposed to the sun
> my wife is beautiful
> my children are healthy

Totally absurd, of course. Tanikawa writes that "I have nothing to write"—a very painful paradox. His privileging of silence finds its purest expression in "Journey 4," where:

> don't move,
> words!
> between me and the sea

Words always cut between things, cut them off. Because words signify by means of that which is not themselves, they continually announce a conclusive distance, a slippage between themselves and that which is not themselves. Language is that which proclaims a disconnection between me and the world, between me and you, even between me and myself. And this distance between me and myself is the beginning of my consciousness of myself, of the misfortune of myself.

After presenting the contradiction between words and silence so eloquently, what words could he still find to speak? This was the difficult question facing Tanikawa in the 1960s and early 70s.

Tanikawa's answer to this question was clear and unequivocal: he would send language out into silence. Although it is true that humans, within language, are unfortunate, and that nature, within silence, is fortunate, it is also true, Tanikawa reasoned, that nature has its own overall economy with its own controlling principles and natural laws. And, if so, then why not liberate words from the self of the poet and let them play freely by themselves? The result was Tanikawa's 1973 *Wordplay Songs*, a book in which words frolic and romp among themselves yet manage to create a world of mysterious beauty. Here is a stanza from the first poem, "I," in which "I" (*watashi*) overlaps and exists within "carry across" (*watasu*) and "ferryman" (*watashimori*):

> I carry across
> carry you across
> carry across to you
> ferryman

This is not the sort of poetry, of course, that can be carried across alive into another language. The meaning survives, but not the body of the words. Not, that is, the silence concealed within the words.

In 1978 Tanikawa's *Fragment of the Apocrypha of Taramaika* was published. It marked a significant expansion of his poetic universe. Words now actively contain silence, while silence strives to contain words.

It is often asserted that Tanikawa and the other poets of his generation rejected philosophical thought, in contrast to the previous generation of poets—symbolized by the Wasteland group—who were deeply interested in politics and society. This notion hardly holds true for Tanikawa, and his works are the best refutation of it. In fact, his poems importantly involve philosophy. Surely this is due to the influence of his father, the philosopher Tanikawa Tetsuzō. Japanese critics have yet to stress this philosophical element in his work. Hopefully Tanikawa will fare better in English.

Tanikawa Shuntarō

The Poems

On the Beach

The land goes on forever.
I can't see the sea.
I can only write the first two lines of a poem
and then it becomes an endless refrain.
Nothing is so hard
that I can't untangle it with words.
I sawed a board,
took some screws, and made a shelf.
This is a fact.
Metaphors have lost their point,
because the world is so broken.
As a boy I read about Medusa
and I remember being scared to death.
Now that I'm stone, though,
nothing scares me.
You see, that's how metaphors are.

That song of waterbirds —
is it a song? a signal?
a bit of information?
None of those, really — only a vibration.
It quickly fans out and is gone.
That is a fact.
This fact takes place only once,
and right now I think that's the only beautiful thing there is.

If there isn't, what'll we do

about the man who's going to die tonight?
If there is,
then what's the point of the future?

It'd be great
if all I had to do was save my soul;
but since other souls are mixed up with mine
I can't even say which soul is mine.

The next morning the phone woke me up.
It was my son and daughter in Tokyo,
who when I said good morning
said good evening.

Written at 14 E. 28th Street, New York City

And W.H. Auden came in, holding a cup of coffee
in his huge hand.
The cup was the aluminum one
he used for brushing his teeth.

And at dinner the night before
someone asked how chopsticks got invented.
"They were suddenly invented in 1910," someone joked.
But no one knows the whole story.

And in a small, empty theater
I watched *The History of Blue Films.*
Some sick ivy clung to a white wall
that had a big crack in it.

Every day one station or another
carried Bach.
My hotel window let in no sunlight,
let alone the sky.

To Mrs. Tamura, who had a cold, we brought home some
raw fish, rice, and pickled radish, in a plastic box.
Marilyn Monroe was alive and well
on TV.

And naturally I kept on signing travelers cheques,
over and over and over.
I wonder if there's any hope for people
as they are?

For John Coltrane

You lived and breathed—that's all;
sighing a thousand times every fifteen minutes.
In your whole life you shouted only once
and, after all, what difference did that make?
I'm going to stop asking these stubborn questions.
At midnight a can of warm beer
and a box of dry crackers—wonder of wonders—
are both our disappointment and our hope.

Well, then, there's only one thing
that can't be expressed
and we don't know if that comes
after we're gone or while we're still alive.

I hear soul and destiny rubbing together.
All I've got now are onomatopoetic words.
But I wonder whether groaning is much use
when it ends up on the printed page.

I close my eyes,
glad not to see visions;
yet some day maybe the fear of that will
drive me crazy.

(February 8, 1973)

At Midnight in the Kitchen I Just Wanted to Talk to You

1.

A couple of junior high kids — a boy and a girl —
are sitting on a bench in the subway station, talking,
grinning like Cheshire cats,
exposing pink gums.

The train swoops in.
I thought they'd get on but they didn't.
Off it goes.
Think of the world in this context.

Why don't you go at it?
I'm too busy thinking about myself
to be interested in you.
I have no time to sit around waiting.

2.
(For Takemitsu Tōru)

As usual, you're out drinking tonight, aren't you?
I hear ice cubes smacking the glass.
I suppose you drone on and on, and suddenly fall silent.
Although there's only one reason for suffering,
people fool themselves in lots of ways.
Do you beat your wife?

3.

(For Oda Makoto)

It's no good blaming the prime minister alone.
He can't even be a symbol.
Your Kansai accent is timeless
but prime ministers come and go.

A shallow brook wheezes through the refrigerator, doesn't it?
I'm drinking coffee here in the kitchen.
Goodness is out of my line
and so I try, at least, to develop good penmanship.

So, tomorrow comes,
overgrown with history,
yet free from history,
and mysteriously arrogant.

Shall I say good morning while it is still night?

4.

(For Tanikawa Tomoko)

I don't blame you for being mad,
because I'm asking you — and I'm not drunk —
to love even the ugliest in me.

There's nowhere to turn.
I guess that like Oedipus I need catharsis —
provided I could still get along
and not be
blind.

What would the chorus chant?
No doubt they'd rise up and shrilly insist,
"Oedipus complex!"

And not without reason.
An interpretation is always just one move too late,
and what I really want is
a ridiculous oracle.

5.

I'm tired of making wise remarks;
tired of talking to the printing press.
I'd like some person—or even a ghost—
to listen to me (though not to respond to everything).

If money could be turned into leaves,
or if maybe half of it could,
then I could sit around all day
just watching the leaves.

It'd be nice if lightning would strike in a bit
and it would rain.
I could even wish for a thief—
that would be preferable to the language of law.

What if a ghost would appear—
maybe young Oiwa's before she was poisoned?
Could I make her happy?

6.

It's not so bad saying nothing.
Anyway he is a sort of cymbal
who when he has howled once or twice
will stay quietly seated.

What'll he do while he's still?
How about keeping bees?
In that case the howling would be about bees.

Though the subject would be bees
I guess he'd really be talking about life—
let him howl.
His tone of voice would be quite different.
How to put it?
His vocal chords, tonsils and tongue are not hard, but thick,

and spit is flying.

7.

I'm going to write you a postcard.
I'll say that I'm fine;
but that's not really true.
I mean, I'm not sick, either.
Truth is somewhere in-between;
neutral, you might say.
But that's the question.
To be neutral?
A silken mass of despair balanced by a speck of leaden hope.
Just like the zoo on Sundays
jammed with people and monkeys.

Anyway, I'm going to write you a card.
I'll drink my Coke and say everything is ok.
Which of us is traveling, though,
gets less and less clear.

In haste . . .

8.
(For Iijima Kōichi)

All of a sudden I was able to write some poems
in this kind of style.
You said that melancholia has keep you in bed,
and I'm still up in spite of depression;
or maybe writing
is what keeps me from getting depressed.
Yet everything is a big bore—
even Mozart.
I'd just like to touch something,
like a plain wood box.
If I could touch it, then I'd caress it; then maybe grab it;
and if I could grab it, than maybe I'd smash it on the floor.
How about you?
How're your fingers?

Is your thumb still your thumb?
Can you wipe yourself?
Poor bastard!

9.

I'm not interested in titles;
making titles is snobbish.
Naturally I am a snob
but right now I'm too busy to mess with titles.

If I had to I'd put down, "Everything," but
"Right Now This is the Best I Can Do" is good enough.
An azalea blooming in the garden is
naturally, unconsciously beautiful.
So then why call my poem "azalea"?

Even though I am writing about the azalea
there're other things on my mind.
There are scads of perfectly terrible Japanese words
and I wish I could set "azalea" free.

The mind is indivisible.

10.
(In the manner of Charlie Brown)

Under the bed there's a pair of comfortable old shoes
and so again this morning I feel like getting up.
Time is actually just like a clock:
it works overtime and never gets bored.

Let's change the subject.

Wind is flowing across the grass.
I see the same old familiar scenery.

It's not easy to change the subject.

11.

Can you hold up this stranger
who is suddenly falling all over you,
puking,
and help him before you wipe the puke off your shirt?

I would hold him
but the moment I did
I'd be picturing that action to myself,
trying to be the first to criticize the picture.

When I got home
I'd puke at the smell of his puke.
It'd be worse than hypocritical.

You might say that
to give this example is itself inexcusable.
But it's already said and done.

Now what?

12.

The pencil I dropped made a terrible sound;
it startled my wife, who was asleep.
I write this
because I have no past to draw on.

Thinking about the past makes me dizzy.
People have spent much too much time thinking
and, honestly, I feel indifferent to all of it.
Yet all by myself I can't conceive a single thing.
In a way I am the sound of the pencil
hitting the floor.
Since the sound has no past, it has no future.

Well,
I just can't keep this up.

13.
(For Yuasa Jōji)

A fountain in Hibiya Park bubbled in seven colors.
Arms extended, a man
stood in the middle of it and got soaked.
A crowd gathered and applauded.
The wind was still wintry.

I sat in an amphitheater until sundown
listening to folk music.
Paper planes were sailing and falling.
A banjo resounded.
Wind shook the tree tops and the songs sounded alike.

Music both hurts and heals;
heals and hurts.

14.
(For Kanaseki Hisao)

Was it Berryman, the suicide,
who sang,
"I have a delicate operation to perform."?
As usual, I don't remember.

I try to disclose myself
but, like a vampire caught in the sun,
as soon as I disclose anything it becomes something else.
Words held back in the soul are nothing at all like
words exposed to air.

Has this ever happened to you?
When you have nothing to say it's because your body is satisfied.
If I couldn't always be like that
then just being dumbfounded would be enough;
wearing a pretty ring;
just being absent-minded.

249

After Shakespeare

Mounted at The Globe, murder and amour.
The curtain opens on a breath-warm boudoir
that leads to a dark corridor and down a creaking staircase
that opens on a quagmire and a blasted wintry heath,
or a vast gray beach—
but the sky is always pure blue.
It's the same story in both hemispheres.
How come the Japanese long ago
lost that noble verse
in which they spoke of the loves of kings?
What mischievous sprite's doing was that?
I'm going to warm up some Campbell's Soup
on the stove.
Not that the future can be told—
since it doesn't contain
a newt's eyeball, dragon scales or a baby's finger.
Even if my birth was Caesarean forty years ago
I can't become a king by killing a kingly regicide.
"Full of sound and fury,
signifying nothing."
What business do I have foisting semantic analysis on such lines?
After you, Shakespeare,
how can I even begin?
It's harder to be a clown than a king.
If I counted up countless abuses
I could still never find a computer to feed metaphors to.
Consider a businessman stepping one-two-one-two
to his 7:40 a.m. commuter train.
A popular kind of 20th century poem answers the sphinx

in complete works of art bought on the monthly installment plan.
Though man has gone to the moon
she is still inconstant.
The world's nothing more than what you see:
a mouth eating soup still swears;
kisses the part you can't say in public;
and at last, unable to breathe,
nourishes white birches under ground.
It's all the same with liars and honest men; silent and talkative.
While opening the creaking night window
I see that my neighbor's tree bears a single persimmon.
Haiku's traditional motif strikes me as simply ripeness
and a seed to consume ripeness.

Where the Sky

When I woke up the whole sky was covered with pomegranates. Sunlight was pouring indescribably to the ground through pale purple pomegranates. Could I explain the mineral halo that each pomegranate wore? The question occurred to me, how are they to be explained? Yet even if one could explain the mechanism of vision there would still remain the ultimate question, 'Why?' The mind, which almost habitually asks why, is finally related to that halo. The world was already there before we acquired sight. This is very irksome, but of course if the world did not exist we couldn't experience irritation.

A monkey-bird flew up from a nearby bush, spiraling its long brown and white tail. I recognized our stupidity in the stupidity of its expression. I wonder whether it has ever gotten around to asking questions? Something in its unique song touches our hearts. It seemed to think that it could peck the pomegranates. It prepared to fly up to the sky just as if it only meant to move to the next tree. Though they appeared to be close-by, the ascending bird could not reach the pomegranates. Until the bird ascended I hadn't realized just how pebble-small it was; only then was I aware of the unaccountable, dignified distance between us and the pomegranates. Finally, it flew out of sight. For some time I kept trying to spot that invisible bird. In just such a way, imagination takes over where sight leaves off, and so I come up against the limitations of sight and doubt the validity of the imagination as an extension of my senses. In the absence of the bird my reflections seemed obscene and ambiguous. No matter how wild I might let my imagination run, it would at some point smack into the wall of language.

That afternoon the roof sang under a raining of pomegranate seeds. Unreasonably curious, I went out and tried catching some but they simply vanished over my head into thin air. The odor of borax hung in the air—nothing more. When we try to catch something our muscles tense because of spatial distortion, which perhaps explains why they vanished. That explanation seemed temporarily to satisfy me. When the raining stopped I looked up and saw that the pomegranates had lost their seeds and had suddenly shrunk into pebbles. I didn't feel the same as I had felt that morning, when my heart had leapt up. I merely have to accept my feelings, which I cannot order about. When my heart muttered that the day had both begun and ended with pomegranates, suddenly, quite unintentionally, I felt grateful.

Shiraishi Kazuko

Shiraishi Kazuko

by Kagiya Yukinobu

Shiraishi Kazuko is one of the few Japanese poets of international renown. This is partly because the translation of a good number of her works have been steadily appearing in English and other foreign languages, and partly also due to the fact that she belongs to the small body of surviving minstrels, and acts out with jazz musicians, both at home and abroad, the drama of collision, entangled competition, harmony and unity of words and music. She frequently gives readings of her own poetry, and her capacity as a performer is unexcelled. Unlike most poets who write their poems closeted in their libraries, she continuously pours her words out in the freedom of the public square. She is a poet with an unusually large repertoire. The open form of her verse expands the subject matter and the subject without reserve and enlarges both the time and the space of her poems. Rather than ossifying the poem's pattern by imprisoning it, on the contrary, she expands the poetic conception and liberates the poem from its claustrophobic world. The supple strength of her ability forms images overflowing with energy, and in addition gives birth to a limitless and infinite vision peculiar to her, realizing a poetic cosmos which is exceedingly unique for a Japanese poet. Her poetic language is naturally vitalized and bestows upon the Japanese language a resilience seldom before seen. Her language exerts an extremely high pressure.

Shiraishi was born in Vancouver. She began writing poems when she was still in her teens and has been writing constantly for more than thirty years now. First she joined the little magazine *VOU*, which was under the direction of Kitazono Katsue, a prominent poet in the center of the Japanese avant garde, and was baptized into modernist poetry. She mastered Kitazono's rigorous rhetoric as well as his refined and perfect techniques. She published her first collection of poetry, *The Town Where Eggs Fall*, in 1951; in it the influence of Kitazono is obvious. Her poetic work dispenses entirely with unnecessary words. She mastered Kitazono's stoic diction and rejects excessive embellishments or metaphors. Kitazono was a modernist poet who enjoyed connections with Ezra Pound, Robert Duncan, Robert Creeley and so forth.

Without falling into modernism's neglect of reality and cleavage from life, Shiraishi sought to press on into a poetic territory peculiar to herself, and succeeded. Just as the poet Terayama Shūji, who also belonged to *VOU*, firmly established his identity, so Shiraishi was able to realize her own personal innovations, while at the same time honoring the immeasurable influence of Kitazono. The resonance of Kitazono's works are still to be heard here and there in her second collection, *Tiger Play*. It is in *Come No Later*, published in 1963, that she finally establishes her own poetic style. Such poems as "Now Is the Time," "Come No Later," "By the Hudson River," "The Several Cats Inside Me In Love With Ornett Coleman's Lonely Woman," and others included in this volume make that quite clear.

The salient characteristic of her sensitivity is the fact that although her medium of expression is linguistic, the roots of her artistic spirit are in modern jazz, art, cinema, contemporary fashion and fads rather than literature and poetry. Among literary artists only Dylan Thomas, Kenneth Rexroth, Allen Ginsberg, Henry Miller, Nishiwaki Junzaburō and Yoshioka Minoru are of her kind. Thomas's emotive power, Rexroth's free life-style, Ginsberg's anti-establishment stance, Miller's exultation of eros, Nishiwaki's celebration of eternity and non-being, Yoshioka's eros which, unlike Miller's, writhes at the bottom of words — these seem to have found resonance in Shiraishi's spirit.

But, more than that, she was strongly attracted to the powers of improvisation of such modern jazz men as John Coltrane, Miles Davis, Eric Dolphy, Charlie Mingus, Albert Eiler and Cecil Taylor. She has a passion, on the order of perfect empathy, for Coltrane's music. In her poem "A Dedication to the Late Coltrane" she writes: "Coltrane/ let me love a day in your life/ as I love you/ let me love the season of a day/ in the forty-one years of life/ you/ lived." She succeeded in swiftly absorbing Coltrane's musicality in the broad sense of the word — the rhythm, the melody, the pulse, the modulation, the breaths and pauses — and in putting it all into living Japanese. The pressure, tension, pitch and uplift of her words are revealed in *Tonight Is Nasty*, and rises to yet another level in *The Season of the Holy Pervert*. She seized on her vision of a "holy pervert" and since has persistently and boldly focused her writing on it.

From around this time she also started pouring into her words the human will to life, and began to freely use the phallus as symbol. Although journalists have called her "the phallus poet" and "the hippie poet" because of her startling images and her ultra-contemporary clothing, she has never been a follower of fads or trends. The eroticism revealed in her works ultimately is always synonymous with the human will to live. This is clearly seen in the group of poems called "A Canoe Returns to the Future."

Shiraishi's work is close to the poetry of Ginsberg and Gregory Corso, and her power to write long, sustained poems is equal to Ginsberg's. Just as "beat poets" sought to be steeped in the holiness of the spirits within them, Shiraishi also reveals a spiritual poetic feeling. At times she over-uses the device of repetition, but repetition often engenders a central rhythm that helps her compose excellent long poems. Although she holds herself to an extremely severe and stoic way of life, she possesses a style which is liquid and plastic.

Her latest work, *Sand Tribe*, is very likely her masterpiece. By adding poetry to insight and contemplation, she creates an imaginary space hidden in desert sand. This collection, though tempered with Confucianism, exults in a belief in the "global poem."

Although her poems are full of western sensitivity, thought, life-style, emotion and customs, she also profoundly realizes the spirituality of the East. Unification of Occident and Orient is central to the method of *Sand Tribe*. Just as Coltrane and Ginsberg were attracted to Indian philosophy and criticised conformist and machine-dominated America, Shiraishi in her recent works since *The Season of the Holy Pervert* calls on the spiritual values of the Orient, even as she writes about her experience of Western ways.

Shiraishi was enthralled by the deep human sadness, the blues, in jazz; she felt in that sadness the roots of human actuality. Basing herself in that vision, and in her own essential innocence, she has succeeded in writing an international poetry while remaining a Japanese poet.

Shiraishi Kazuko

The Poems

Under The Blue Sky   A Boy   A Funeral
(from *Sand Tribe)*

Somebody is watching from a window
I am in a sanctuary
The blue sky is falling down   looking up I
Go head over heels toward that blue sky
Around where the blue sky hangs low
     are white-walled crumbling houses   out of the
Second floor window of one somebody is
Watching   I want one of those boys
In dirty dusty robes to put in my
     pocket
And   to let him walk near the corners of the
     heart-covering square   in
My heart covered with sandy dust   which seems
     also an endless square   now
     nobody is playing
Hopscotch   nor is there a dove nor a sparrow nor
     a hawk nor Horus   a space
A void
The sanctuary where I am is
At the bottom of a hollow in the ground
Probably four floors deep down
So I who stand in a garden of the
     sanctuary am like
An animal in a cageless square hole
     in a safari park   but
I have no fangs   no brutality   I am
     positively tame

Bathed in sun   if I might   I would
    like to fall into a doze
But   the blue sky too radiant comes falling
    down from heaven
To ward it off I must wear glasses the
    colour of grass
otherwise   the blue sky   could come
    falling onto the verge of my stomach
    my heart
And dye me pure blue

A boy is peeking   out of the window
There are paneled walls covering the environs
    of the sanctuary from above and
From among them a white house protrudes
Out of the top floor window of this three-storey house
    a boy   his head now revealed   looks
    somewhere
One moment in the boy's fifty or seventy years
    of life is
Now stuck on the verge of the window

I   go in and out of the sanctuary
Go into a courtyard   go into a back yard
The sheep god with curly horns is my relative
I cannot but greet him
A brief conversation   2000 years in a glance
    long time no see
But   I hear the music   four five   and
    ten year old poor kids suddenly appear
Their obscene dances songs and abuses are full of
    innocent malice
Their pranks begin   tambourine in hand
    a skirt lifted lewdly
Earrings shaken   smeared nostrils flaunted
    white teeth flashed   curiousity
    affability and cunning in the corners
    of the eyes   playing primitive instruments
Covered with dust   on a river bank   looking down
    on the sanctuary   they dance

They are poor   obscene   beautiful gods
Filled with malice   realists on the earth
     transfigured into illusionary children
A musical scale on its way to yet un-attained
     maturity
Does not stay in tune and   in the off-key blue
     sky
Hangs like laundry

Then
On the opposite bank near the walls
Men chance to pass by
Grim faced   to offer a prayer
Grim faced   with no sign of a smile
Or jest
Without tears
In a great sound of silence   reciting something
Men
With a corpse   on rigid cloth
A blanket draped over it
Four men holding   the four corners
March on

The blue sky   falls down   on the funeral
Clearing it off   and off
Covered   with blue sky
By midday sun   burnt to the shoulders
Carrying the corpse   on rigid cloth
     reciting prayers
In the rustic town   Ezna   from one white house
     to another
From one alley   turning into another alley
Through the street next to the sanctuary
     where the paneled walls are crumbling
On they march
In the distance   or   in the neighbourhood
Wherever it is   to a burial ground

Sunday 26 November   Arrive in Cairo
Room 124   Shepherds Hotel
Afternoon   visit the Egyptian Museum to meet
That man
Hall of mummies   several dozen king's corpses
Mingling with the coffins of their relatives

Slowly   in broad daylight
From a coffin   an illusory shadow rises
It is that   man

King Khufu   or   Amenhotep
Ramesses the III or someone else   although I try
to read that man's name
No matter how many times I read it   the coffins
appear different and
Until the end I can not verify
Who he is

With a mummy   to leave a coffin with a king
At this moment   several dozens I's
Wearing jackets of lamè blue
In a coffin   forcibly rise to their feet
With the king   and the several dozen I's who
now have just woken from the coffins
I walk in the streets of Cairo
My thoughts in perfumed oil
Gradually amplifying at the trickle of Koran's tongue
Go to the River Nile and perform ablution

Monday 27 November   No sandstorm
I was given a ship of papyrus by my uncle
It is in fact a ship drawn on a sheet of papyrus
setting sail in white
About to emerge
Upon which   Nubian men   are bustling about
A boat   which has been asleep in my pocket
At that moment   with a faint sound of running
water at the gunwales   wakes up
A ship calls for a boat?

The boat has gone nowhere   it is within me
My offing is dark   or a haze hangs there and
At times   the ship   becomes totally
Invisible to me

What goes running   beyond that yellow desert is
Not twelve camels but
Several dozen
I's
Who rise up from the coffin
To the dancing of twelve I's   upon the dry
      air of the Sahara
Twelve I's   on camel back   or
On foot go running into the desert   it is
Not a sense but a rhythm   an erection

I realise I have been looking for the boat
      ever since
Tuesday 28 November
En route from Cairo to Alexandria
I was in search of a sail
Noticing a sail along a bus route
As if catching a butterfly in a net
I took a picture
I am now a sail huntress   a poacher
Not that I was out for sails
I had collected nearly everything related to boats
      but
The beautiful boy   I did not catch
Named Asser Mohammed wearing the blue sea
I found him in the alley in front of the museum
In Alexandria by the Mediterranean Sea and
Without collecting lips   nor chastity
I let him go   back to the sea

West is the country of the dead
      West is the country of the dead
M recites that like beads
However   I like

This town of the dead   beat their wings of
        black cloth
In this town of the dead   a jar shop is breaking
        down faster than death
A cloth shop is going on with an obscene prattle
        taste indecent and vulgar
I like the unenlightened power   dreadful crowd
Swarming there like flies
Both S and I are black ravens now   flocking
Only   upon the demon cloth   rippling
        flooding over the road
Of hundreds of thousands of brilliant colours
        totteringly   flocking
Then at the moment   the madness within ourselves
Hits the key of climax
Nearly   becoming the ecstasy of an ancient carpet
        we
Rend each others' cerebra into shreds

Wednesday 29 November
Arrive in Luxor PM 2:00
The sun is still right over our heads and
Into the window of room 38 at the Luxor Hotel pour
Tens of hundreds of voices of birds from the garden
Despite the absence of a bathtub   warm water
        slowly runs within me
The dead resurrected from the coffins   and several
        dozen I's alike   turning into light cells
        perform ablutions in the warm water

Thursday 30 November
I stand at the entrance
Everybody talks of entering but I refuse
In the direction of a rock mountain under the blue
        sky   I see that man go walking
A mummy with a Kha in the heat of the day
But for a walk
Upon the hill above   a little way from the Valley of
        the Imperial Family

I am not entitled to disturb his silence
Nor his calm thoughts nor his amusement

Slowly rising up from the coffins
Twelve doubles who are myself
Begin to stroll over the hill each in its own way
At which   somebody   says   water!
And I   stretch   out
Hundreds of thousands of tens of thousands of spirits
        in sunlight excessively strong
Are drying an extremely tender part of their
        souls
What we call "a tear" is not becoming to
        this land
All water flushing in the throat and
In an instant   I   empty a flask

Whose voice is it that said water!
Sounds as if it came from thousands of years ago
        but
The sound of water   has become a cascade and
Falls in a rush to the bottom of my throat

Friday 1 December
I stand at the sanctuary
Over my head   suddenly
The blue sky comes falling down

Sunday 3 December   Absimbel
The Nile becomes the sea in the end   from a river
        to a lake   to an enormous sea
Dark rocks now crocodiles turn up but
Here it is   the upper Nile   sands from the land
        of yellow sand
Animating in the heated colour of pink   at length
        turn into pink sands

Saturday 2 December
Buggy drivers

Gathered on a sheepskin rug in a circle in broad
    daylight
Bite into cheese and drink spirits
When night comes   they invite us home
A white horse and a donkey live in a hall in the
    middle
In the little chambers around it
Several men are gathered
Take my wife   tonight if you please
The man   wants to give everything   to a guest
    from afar
He's a nice fellow so
At a house with an old mother a wife children and
    chickens without a roof   from where
A crescent moon and stars can be seen
He is devoted to the pleasure of his guests
On the way back home   catching a chicken to
    pluck its feathers he
Hands me a plume for my hair

Going back along the road of starry skies
He keeps talking about man's love but
I
Think of the torso of a Nubian man on the boat
    I boarded in the daytime
This is not love but desire
I-miss-you for delicious things but
The man keeps on talking about man's friendship and love
    while
I think of the scene where a Lagazza
Erect as a log   sets sail   on a boat
Man and boat
Which is the more heart-rending scene
I do not know
In the Nile within myself crocodiles with fluttering
    hearts
Raise   the sound of waves   beat the gunwales with
    the sounds of water

Somebody is watching from the window
I am in the sanctuary
The blue sky is falling down
A boy alone
Somewhere from a high window is peeking and
The funeral march has just passed
The phantom that rose from the coffin
With me   is watching
The burial of somebody   who died yesterday
Once dead   will not die   twice
Yet   there is something which rises   slowly
From a coffin   many times
For instance   that man   and I myself
Before becoming sunstruck
Slyly   I   get into a coffin
To feign sleep
Several dozens of years   and at times   several
      thousands of years   how long
Will my poesy   go on with sleeping
Listening   and watching
The blue sky is falling down   the funeral
      march is passing by
Within me   yet again
Something is resurrecting

To give it shape
In haste I
Board flight 876 departing Cairo
Monday 5 December
Blue sky
Blue sky
Under the blue sky a boy and shapes without name
Appear all the more real for being buried
Appear all the more real for being buried

My Sand People
(from *Sand Tribe*)

He is one of the sand people   a descendent of
     my sand clan
A desert stuck to his eyes
Since the day he came back from Saudi Arabia
Come rain or shine
At the back of his eyes a cloud of dust rises
A camel brays
In his eyes a horizon stares at
     eternity
At long last he has taken to living at the heart
     of sand hot and taciturn as the
     merciless blazing sun
His spirit sups sand as if it were porridge
He is marrying into the family
Of that vast existence named desert
His bride?
Not the Koran   the sand
The spirit called sand clan now
Has gulped down the setting sun
His stomach is horizontal and will never
     disturb the horizon

Mr T who returned from Saudi Arabia the other
     day
Brought me an eyeball the colour of water
     blue
The false eye of Lawrence of Arabia

Do not ask if he had
        a false eye
My tongue and eyes to tell you the truth are
        illusion
So as to taste the absence of real
        images
Pointing at a chart   Here was the office of Lawrence
Now being destroyed it will be rebuilt
Sand spills where his index finger points
        on the chart
The chart is made of sand and the names are men's
Nostrils dreamy visions
More precisely   only sand has an address
Men are not even wind furrows nor merely drifting
        sands

My sand people
He is one of the sand people
The desert sticks to his eyes and from time to
        time
Sand rises to conceal the expressions on his face
Is he crying or smiling?
At such moments
I strain my ears to listen to
The dripping of water
Hitting the bottom of a bathtub
That I once heard in room 306 in the Continental Hotel
        in Cairo
The faucet was broken and in regular rhythm water
        dripped
Outside the room the evening prayer of the Koran and
        the voices of a crowd
Upon a soft bed
In a stone-walled room like a coffin I laid my body
        down
Soft and alive   held myself still
Like the dead like an ancient king in a 5000 year
        sleep
I too have let the yellow sand storm live in
        my eyes

Not a seasonal wind that only blows in March
But one which blows in all seasons
At least while I am alive
Inside at the entrance of the spirit
Since the day of Mr T brought me the false eye of
        Lawrence of Arabia
I have learned that the Sahara in contiguous
With the man who spent 200 hundred days sticking
        boards on the ceiling
During the construction of the Saudi Arabian
        Imperial Palace
The desert of the rumination into which I stepped
        to know
Myself a Sphinx
the sand people is

What
Did I see in the false eye of Lawrence?
A universe made of aqua blue   a romance
Transparent yet all absent
For such reasons it reflects anything
Can become anyone
What has he become?
Whether he likes it or not
Almost as if for love he buried half his
        his life in the sand
His spirit buried in the sand
He returned to London with one less eye for
        seeing

Mr T has got eyes
They are not false eyes
Alive and undulating   looking like the sea
They are sands   they are deserts
Where does the wind come from
That blows over the desert without pause?
The eyes of Mr T   like a Radar
        catch it
In this instance   the wind is a god
Or should I call it a devil

That office was in the centre of Jeddah
Sometimes I went for a drive
And as he speaks the wind runs into his
        eyes
Several dozen of years have passed since
        Lawrence's death and
Here is Mr T his heart breaking at the age
        of 25
Here he is
Although there is neither a revolution nor
        a war around now
The infallible sun
With repetitive severity crawls along the ground
To scorch men
Should you carelessly lose your passport and
        get locked up
You'd be flirting with death   not just sunstroke
There's no roof down there you know
Ra   there is only the sun

I remember the afternoon of that day
The blue sky permeated
A boy was looking out of the window on the
        third floor of a house with white
        plastered walls
The blue sky permeated   permeated my brain
Into me who was at the bottom of the Ezna
        shrine
Without mercy sun upon sun caved in
Silently I swallowed them one after another
A moment afterward   I saw
Sturdy men   the dead carried on a
        board of canvas   without tears
        their eyes fixed straight in front
Heading for a place of burial I do not know
        where
I saw them walking
Their voices deep and low in prayer
Toward the burial place   I know not where
I saw the funeral march pass

After the funeral march dispersed
There was the desert   they had left it intact
The Sphinx slept all day long
Or with eyeless eyes looked into eternity
Nothing there   but the sands
It is the desert

While I was in a coach driving beside the Nile
To the Karnak temple   amid the obscene chattering
          of coachmen
The wind glistened and bent   flew in
          through the window
The wind
Was it not the same wind that
Swiftly turned
On the afternoon in deserted Jeddah
And disappeared?

The glistening wind comes into   goes out of
          my eyes like a silhouette
Like a bird in black

There were no women there
Only a black veil flickering from time to time
At noon before resting
He would dive into the sea behind the
          factory
And then without haste
His spirit would begin to sup on the sand
          as if it were gruel
The hearts of the taciturn sand people
Living on the sand
Realize Zen in the void
In his eyes he has a horizon that stares at
          eternity and
He lets the numerous blazing suns
Sleep within his heart of sand
Voices of the Koran
The braying of camels

Sounds of water
Songs of birds
Pass by
As do the winds

Ra (the sun king)
The sheep god
Isis
Each of them
Kisses toward eternity
Sands are generous to them
The spirits of the sand never cease to
        embrace them
They comprehend with their bodies
        eternity on earth

Lawrence's false eye remains transparent
Even in the sandless city where concrete
        breeds
Because of its absence
It reflects all   never becomes tarnished
Sand people
He   Mr T   phantom eyes inside me

They are all sand people
The desert which stares at the horizon
        all day long
Is stuck there where a cloud of dust
        rises and
The spirit of the sand   drawing invisible
        sutras upon occasion
Ascends into the Heavens

I Wonder If You Were Tooting Bec

I wonder if you were Tooting Bec
I wonder if you were a rose
You are aren't you a large-petalled pink rose
With the 6:30 evening sun shining on you?
No not 6:30
8:30
It stays light until 9:00

It's right to call you Tooting Bec Gardens
And it's right to call you No.55 in that street
You're the south side of London
I've not made love with you
What did you think of
Those West Indian black brothers who showed up at the
        pool side
The younger one wanted to fuck in a bush at the back
And made a violent tackle but
The older one just looked on serenely
Serene intelligence
From firm buttocks
Slim legs all serene and
Barely keeping his 23 years
In check before they went mad with passion
Why am I suddenly reminded of
Late September in Tokyo
Of the slightly lonely sunlight on the rose
Large-petalled pink rose
It was summer but the autumn sunlight in
An immature summer failing to be summer

Or she
Went out of the door to start her life
On a bus
Or she might have taken a bus from this life
To the beginning of another life
Young as she was she spread
Both arms to receive the autumn sunlight
It must be called resolution
In a country without summer people no matter how
       young they are
Have to lead lives
That allow for autumn in its entirety

Suddenly an amusement park turned up in a bush
Coming only in the summer like a circus on
       wheels
The Travelling Amusement Park's neon glimmers in
       vivid colours and
From the neighborhood on motorcycles in automobiles
       and on bicycles
The naughty teenagers came
Turn turn not a roundabout but a big wheel
Run run dodgem cars in an electric arena
Miss U and David too are Micky Mice
Riding the dodgems

Did it really exist London Tooting Bec?
After a storm had past
Was the large-petalled pink rose still blooming
       as it did in summer

8:30 was nothing but a joke
The rose was so large
It exceeded reality
Became an illusion
What would become of a flower so small
       a buttercup?

After the gardener came to prune the rose
An old ruined aristocratic homosexual
His beloved cat in his arms
Smoothing down his white hair
Grumbled to everyone about an atrocious landlord

Are you Tooting Bec?
Even without a buttercup
You are Tooting Bec
An illusionary large-petalled rose in arms
Correcting 6:30
To 8:30
I wonder if you were a
Spirit
Living at the No.55
Tooting Bec Gardens of summer time
Within me

(We haven't made love, have we?)

Yoshimasu Gōzō

Yoshimasu Gōzō

by Iijima Kōichi

I first noticed Yoshimasu Gōzō when his second book, *Gold Poems*, came out in 1970. It was an historic event in modern Japanese poetry.

A number of strict taboos controlled prewar Japanese poetry, especially poetry written after 1926, when the Showa era under emperor Hirohito began. One was against shouting and exclaiming; another was against running or moving at top speed. Poets then thought of themselves as gardeners, trimming and adjusting phrases and words rather than expressing their feelings directly and revealing the turmoil and utter chaos that actually underlay and sustained their poems in spite of all their efforts at immaculate surface control. It's true that some poets presented a facade of swaggering and heroic posing, but their poems were rarely the result of spiritual struggle and power. Yoshimasu Gōzō is not a gardener. He has a sensitivity to deep rhythms that allows him to endure the wildest screams, speed, midair collisions. He writes in long, arcing cadences and lines that explode like water at the bottom of a waterfall, bursting and boiling back up in sounds that are always more than simply noise. His music can't be accounted for.

A couple of examples will show the terrain over which Yoshimasu climbed on his way to *Devil's Wind*:

> Morning
> running
> when I get to the window

> the tide's up to the second floor
> rocks running
> shadows running   Tokyo
> souls running
> running   geneology of a scream
> this hell
> I confess precisely
> from Shinjuku to Kanda
> when this paper touches air it burns

Even these few lines from "Running Wild" show how hard and how long Yoshimasu has been running. Almost thirty years ago he wrote "The Child Who Can't Stop Running," and he continues to move forward as if he were possessed. Because he is possessed. He runs as no Japanese poet ever has before. In "Gold Rope in Morning Mist" he sets out with "you," his car: "Today / careening through morning mist / we chase a huge, final landscape, a scene off a picture scroll of Buddhist paradise / west, west / riding the Contessa S / 6 A.M., September 19, 1967 / mist over the whole Musashino plain / we cut across rows of keyaki trees / run out of control, you and I, held together by a gold rope / both of us flying / the fields are music / running, running, running / when I finish this poem / watch my face closely / and pity it." Then: "Your purple shutters are blast furnaces / people will call it masturbation / but this pleasure is my only sexuality   and yours. . . ."

2.

When Yoshimasu came out with *Devil's Wind* in 1979, he showed he was able to leap not only behind himself but also behind contemporary Japanese culture, with its air-conditioned version of the ice age.

In the long poem "Cradle," he lulls us with loneliness:

> I want to live quietly, growing eggplants in a vacant
>   lot—, my soul shudders.
> High wind warning for the north Japan Sea—,
>   fishermen, please be careful.

Growing eggplants. It is Rimbaud, it is the ancient Chinese recluse poet T'ao Ch'ien. Poets have always been tempted by this life. But in the air conditioned age, in polluted modern Tokyo, a young poet singing like this? Then down dives his roaring, shuddering soul. From the beginning Yoshimasu has been obsessed with souls. At first I wasn't impressed, but after I visited Miyako Island in the Ryukyus, where spirits and shamanesses and goddesses still live, I learned to take souls more seriously. Several experiences since then have taught me that Yoshimasu's soul-storm is no fiction.

> High wind warnings for the north Japan Sea—,

It caught me by surprise. And then "fishermen, please be careful" trapped me with its tenderness. I don't like to use the word lightly; but this line shows us the other side of Japan today. The age of tenderness.

Another line winding in and out of "Cradle" always astonishes me with its commitment to the tiny sounds of history:

> I've heard there are hospital ships—, is one in
> the bay?

Yoshimasu was only a child during the war, and the ships were a distant legend. Yet he pulls the past through the present and anchors it in a blind spot in our air. Not many contemporary Japanese poems have lines that suddenly lift the reader this way, although the compressed seventeen syllables of a haiku are still sometimes able to.

> The magic walk goes on.

Yoshimasu makes people take this walk with him. And hear again at close range the name of a famous swimming champion:

> Mr. Furuhashi Hironoshin.

The name runs through me like an electric shock, quickly followed by:

> I DON'T KNOW WHY.

It cuts suddenly like the shaft of a searchlight, which, turning, reveals some of pride-hungry postwar Japan's most seductive fantasies.

Yoshimasu's style in *Devil's Wind* is marked above all by courage and endurance.

> Be quiet   I'm rushing to   the exit —, magic marks,
>   catch your breath.

You, I want you born — but someone's breaking
    apart   hanging in air
— again just so   Ma   again   Mama   rice   rushing
    to the exit   emotions in my arms   I stare out
    at the cosmos

It takes confidence to swing this high, to hang from an unknown and unknowable region. Reading "Cradle" changes your breathing, your heartbeat. It is a world of reversed images, a negative world, a world of fear.

        There's a world in side mirrors   we can't know it

I like to read this long poem slowly and quietly. In it are traces of a journey, by Orpheus, by Bashō, by three decades after the war, by a contemporary Japanese poet, which may not be looked back on safely. A man runs through the dark holding out a stick. This stick is his only protection, tapping, making desperate holes in the wind. The great many punctuation marks, spaces, and dashes in *Devil's Wind* are holes opened by his stick. This discovery gives Yoshimasu the length and scale he needs.

This long poem is slowly shattering Yoshimasu's heart. We who read *Devil's Wind* on the printed page hear it only quietly. I still remember the first time I heard Yoshimasu give one of his unique "readings." It took him more than forty minutes to get through "Cradle" and part of "Ema" in what was a trance-song rather than what is usually meant by a poetry reading. When he chanted, from "Ema,"

COSMO MORE WAS SWAYING   A MAZDA COSMO WAS SWAYING
    TOO WAS SWAYING

he was on the border of another world than sanity. Cosmo, the name of a Mazda car model, had become cosmos, had become peaches (*momo*), had become thighs (*momo*). In Yoshimasu's long voice all four were having sex with each other. The great swoopings of his emotions threatened me, attacked me, finally terrorized me. Then, when it was over, he came and sat down and smiled softly at me.

Yoshimasu Gōzō
The Poems

from Cradle: a Thousand Steps
(from *Devil's Wind*)

The magic walk goes on. Sunset, my spirit and I go forth. Through the escape hatch. I start wandering the cosmos. Long since I lost my ticket, but within my body I still feel a strange energy. Fluting sound, and the escape hatch. I am moving through a crowd. (I, between man and wóman.) Sunset, my spirit and I go forth.

      I'll put
         /through a call
              /to you
                      /from outside

      this is
      /home
           land.

      there
         /is a
            PED
         XING,

moon

a puzzle
  /surfaces
  there
too

I would rather stay in a room in the city   listening
              to the radio.

I'm a magnetic field   maybe I'm deaf   in this corner
              of reality

Neither revolutionary nor patriotic   But   staring
              at a strange passion   at an empty box _____.

Inside a circus land   lions and elephants   clowns
              beautiful girls _____.

There's a land of left-side mirrors   I don't know it _____.

Puzzling land   I don't know how long ago the black
              student uniforms started floating   a corpse
              floats on the lake _____.

This is a land of codes   a floating log on which
              a spirit drifts   the second hand moves round
              three billion times _____.

One eye closed   and looking into the distance   see
              the mouth of Hades   it's like a flute _____.

Once   in a strange land   the mailbox was a flute
                    now   in the age of pay phones   they
                    are proud of the change.

_____, the earth is wet   like a river bottom   raincoats
                    are in fashion

This is a land of codes   where is the colony   a sheet
                    of white paper comes to mind _____, *ne*.[1]

Planting an eggplant on empty land   I want to live
                    quietly _____.
                    ne. My spirit is in turmoil.

There's a high wind warning off Sanriku _____, fishermen
                    please be careful.

Oh   Wind _____.

Right now I'm making tracks on a page   a sheet of blank
                    airmail paper _____, quietly _____,

This is a land of codes, quietly trespassing on
                    Waterworks Bureau land   coming out
                    the back gate, _____ water _____.

    A brook
            /flows

    down
    mainstreet
            /in the
            capital.

Odd that the Waterworks Bureau is here. There's a (gate), sometimes a (secret passage), I can smell fear. You can't use the escape hatch here. I'm sneaking around like someone who retired years ago, going over the (back gate).

This land of codes   numbers chalked on the blacktop
                the limestone mountain is shrinking _____.

_____, the coal-laden   freight train disappears   a memory
                of snow remains   like a withered leaf

At the freight station   where lines tangle   a white
                ball   surfaces.

The pelvis aches   looking at the clear night sky
                the planet turning _____.

White ball   moving oddly   like the cast-off skin
                of an undercover agent   a real estate agent,

The magic walk goes on. Sunset, my spirit and I go forth. There is an escape hatch, I start wandering in the cosmos. Long since I lost my ticket, but within my body I still feel a strange energy.

        Any
        /river

Mud puddle, lake water, shining like window glass, skirt flapping in the wind, window cleaner's platform, cable that scuttles through space, underneath, a motorcycle cop scuttles by

I have nothing to say, infinitely, infinitely, maybe I'm,
                empty-headed

Planting an eggplant on empty land I want to live quietly
   my spirit is in turmoil.

There's a high wind warning off Sanriku _____. Fishermen
   please be careful.

Oh Wind _____.

Could it be I'm deaf an immaculate conception and
   red light flashing a window waving a hand

Could it be a falsetto the bare bulb in the autopsy room
   swing-ing _____,

Well _____ I snapped a picture _____ I snapped a picture _____

The magic walk goes on. Sunset, my spirit and I go forth. There is the excape
hatch, I start wandering in the cosmos. Long since I lost my ticket, but within my
body I still feel a strange energy.

  There is
  /the escape hatch,
   there

   I go forth
  with
  my spirit.

From a window seat on a Keio bus a mountainside
   I breathed the fresh air

 This is a land of codes a land of body warmers
   tobacco Grandma _____.

   Won't you breathe it in?

  That evening I got a phone call from Mt. Yatsugatake
   that inspired me.

I wrote a letter to the 6000 year-old *Jōmon*[2] children _____,
        to the inspiration inside the magnetic field _____,

   The eyes
   /of the dice

   are
   /sunset.

_____ What will turn up?

Along with the doctors   the patients cast dice
            the hallway is _____ dim,

Hazy back alley of a hospital complex   I   too
            am an upflung scalpel _____

Waving a hand   that window   flashing red light
            immaculate conception.

   The privilege
   of walking/
   do you/
   have a right

   to walk.

Well.

_____What will turn up?

Well.

_____, morgue _____.

The magic walk goes on. Sunset, my spirit and I go forth. There is an escape hatch,
I start walking in the cosmos. It's long since I lost my ticket, but within my body I
still feel a strange energy.

There's something called a hospital ship
                    I once heard _____, docked at an inlet?

Why are there so many pharmacies and clinics _____,

It's like a tidal path   like a hallway   walking along
                    rough underfoot   too   well

                    ne.

I've wandered the back alley of a hospital complex
                    docked _____ at which inlet

_____ Hospital ship   I don't know that ship
                    I don't know about hallways

There's a wall that sticks in my mind   won't leave
                    a post card looks like that

        Well.

The privilege
of walking
      do you
      have a right

to walk.

Green wheels and white papers emerging from scarlet, this is the way we head towards midsummer, 1977. I pray to God. Writing some pages in a notebook, the mind's shape opening to the peninsula, now I'm going to write about the coming of the mysterious season. The sea is a wheel, the waves are fossils, the sea wheel becomes a syringe and penetrates the beach, the mind's shape is the waves' crashing, I go down to the sea.

Mud puddle, lake water, shining like window glass, skirt flapping in the wind, window cleaners platform, cable scuttling through space, underneath, a motorcycle cop scuttles by _____.

TO THE HOUSES THAT ARE BOXES OF
THE SPIRIT, MORTAR WALLS, MORTAR
CRACKS, MORTAR WALLS, MORTAR
CRACKS, I AM, A THING THAT LIVES
IN THE CRACKS, NOT ONE THAT LIVES
ON RANCHES OR IN FORESTS. UNDER
STAND? YOU CANNOT LEAVE THE CITY.

GOD, DEVIL, FOXY LADY, WHO COMES
TO THE STATION, I AM, A THING
THAT LIVES IN THE CRACKS, NOT
ONE THAT LIVES ON RANCHES OR
IN FORESTS. GET THAT? YOU
CANNOT LEAVE THE CITY.

WELL, GET THAT, COMES TO THE
STATION, TIGER CARGO, OR, FOXY
LADY.

TO THE HOUSES THAT ARE BOXES
OF THE SPIRIT, MORTAR CRACKS,
FROM SOMEWHERE, YOU CAN, HEAR
IT, THE VOICE, OF AN OLD, WOMAN
WELL, GET THAT, COMES TO THE
STATION, TIGER CARGO, OR, FOXY
LADY.

I will
    /put through a call
    /to you
      from outside

People from the land of woes, and people from Tokyo Elec-
            tric came too   cast up a white ball in the hallway

Goya putting on beautiful clothes   trampoline!

The land of the theater,   I did   not walk   but I will step
          on it   *a thousand steps*.

Planting an eggplant on empty land   I want to live quietly
          ne   my spirit is in turmoil.

There's a high wind warning off Sanriku _____ fishermen
          please be careful.

Oh   Wind _____.

From a puzzling song   to a magic song _____ Tokyo
          is the exit for the spirits, the homeland's

Wind _____.

_____, _____, _____,
 _____, _____, _____,
  _____, _____, _____,

        is
        a beast land
             evil

        wipe it out

Planting an eggplant on empty land I want to live quietly
                    ne   my spirit is in turmoil.

Oh Wind _____.

        Wipe it out!
        Evil
             beast
             land

        code
        all those god
        damned signs

        goddam it

        _____

        /_____,

        _____

298

————————,
/————————.

Bare bulb.
     /goddamn
      it!

There is an escape hatch, I start wandering in the cosmos. Long time since I lost
my ticket, but within my body I still feel a strange energy. A fluting sound, and
the escape hatch. I am moving through a crowd (I, a being between man and
woman.)   Sunset, my spirit and I go forth.

This box
    /is
    /full
    /of
    /in-
    finity.

WEATHER FORECAST AND SHORT WAVE
VOICES ARE AUDIBLE. GET THIS,
COMES TO THE STATION, TIGER CAR-
GO, FOXY LADY. THIS IS WHAT I
TAPED, THIS, WINTER, THESE SOUNDS
OF A STRANGE VOICE. NOT, A SONG,
AT ALL.

Northern Japanese windchime.

Spirits   take a memo
        post war records

At the north end of my spirit   there is a box.

      COULD MY VOICE BE RECORDED.

      I'M PROTECTING MY HEAD FROM THE SNOW WITH
      A BASEBALL CAP.   BUT I DON'T HAVE A ZIP
      CODE OR (OTHER) NUMBER ON MY BACK.   GOD,
      ERASED THE NUMBER.   I CAN'T LIVE, EVEN IN
      AN IGLOO.   I BROUGHT A COFFEE CUP, AND,
      SOME INSTANT COFFEE.   BESIDES, I'M NOT
      COPYING, A WANDERING, PILGRIM.

. . . .

      COULD MY VOICE BE RECORDED

. . . .

      WHITE SPACE

. . . .

      FRAGMENTS

. . . .

The magic walk goes on. My spirit and I go forth. There is an escape hatch, I start
wandering.

Planting an eggplant on empty land I want to end my life
            quietly _____ my spirit is in turmoil.

There's a high wind warning off Sanriku _____ fishermen
          please be careful

Oh Wind _____.

300

There's a time for emptiness   it's like sitting   staring
              into God's eyes   Do I really exist?

Mind is

box.

Explosion.

(A STRANGE SOUND REACHES ME.)

Probably I won't be looking in any more dictionaries.

(A MAGICAL FLUTING   YOU CAN HEAR IT)

10:17.   Old clock.

(THE COSMOS IS TERRIBLY QUIET.)

Mr. Hironoshin Furuhashi.

I DON'T KNOW WHY.

One footnote.

Last summer   I caught something like inspiration
           dolphin's words from offshore.

Feeeeeeeeeee

Or a nuclear submarine   grade school   high school
                    swimming pools   land markers.

An island location.

Mr. Hironoshin Furuhashi.

(A STRANGE FIXER.)

10:25.   Old clock.

The surface of the moon shall turn to blood.
                    Revelations   6

                    Abortion.

(I am NOT WRITING.)

          I
          am a
          CAPITAL
          LETTER

          There
          /at the escape
          hatch   ,
                  I go forth
          with
                  my spirit.

          There is a
          /PED
          XING

          I cross it.

Oh, casting off, the cicada's shell, the first page of summer memories, once upon a time, August was parading. It is an undercover agent's cast-off skin, this white ball, still making strange movements.

The pelvis aches   looking at the clear night sky
                the planet turning _____.

At the freight station   where lines tangle
                a white ball surfaces.

Casting off   the cicada's shell   the first page of summer
                memories   the red light still flashing

A car antenna   traffic report comes in   long-haul trucker.

Diagonal, crossing absolutely prohibited unless otherwise specified.

Diagonal, crossing, is not, allowed, whirlpools, are not, allowed, *prruuufeeee*, offshore dolphins, you must not, go into, the fishing zone.

Shouldn't, do it, cicada's shell, too, white ball, too, telephone wires, too, get this, boing, boing, comes to the station, tiger cargo, foxy lady, in the crowd, crossing, absolutely prohibited.

Spirits   must not expose   the first page of
                summer memories.

        Apollo's
        /narrow
        detour _____,
        Raccoon Hill

take
your coat
off,
    there

/

cut and fill.

it's
Apollo's escape
hatch.

      GOD, DEVIL, OR, COMES TO THE STATION,
      TIGER CARGO, TRAIN, FOXY LADY, BEHOLD
      ONE WHO LIVES AMONG THE CRACKS, NOT
      ONE WHO LIVES ON RANCHES OR IN FORESTS.
      GET THAT, YOU CANNOT LEAVE THE CITY.

thing that lives among the cracks   I am the one   who
      is playing   in the street jumping   elastic
      twist   at a narrow corner   deep in the city

A wind swirls on the blacktop   powder snow
      night in early March

Air twists into cracks in the cosmos   the search
      for a lover begins.

      That, month's issue, didn't list, your,
name. I tried opening several kinds of calen-
dars, certain pages, but your name, wasn't,
there. I bought, a year's horoscope, and
flipped through some pages, but there was,
no, description, of you. Your name wasn't
on the copyright notice page. Anxious, I
thought, you might have changed, your
hairdo, so I went to several coffee shops,

304

pushed on their doors, I think I did. It
seemed, I, just pushed on air, my fingers
slipping on the shape, of your hairdo, maybe.
Anyway.

That, month's issue, didn't list, your,
name. Turning pages of pictures, showing
spirits, standing before, the houses' doors, I
knew from long ago, a second-hand book-
store, probably, had that month's issue, so I
checked, then finally touched, a naked body,
that didn't cast a shadow. It was always the
same, even in a philosophy magazine, the
same thing happened. Faintly, deep inside
that month's issue was the shape of a god-
dess, Demeter, when I was, flipping
through. But it was there, too, like a staple,
hidden in the spine, of a book. Like a seam,
a strange light, shining from the gutters.

That, month's issue, was probably,
secretly, at a bookbinder, where someone

's hand had made a partial change, it seemed.
The strange thing was that the staple, was,
an old nail. Right then, a birdlike shadow,
crossed, by the shadow of a rock. There was
the smell of humus, and a stain, too, like a
footprint, and I was caught in a feeling of
despair.

That, month's issue, didn't list, your,
name. It was not to be found, even in an
address book. It was snowing. A little out of
season for March. And still, I was visiting
coffee shops, pushing on doors, walking,
looking for your name, which should be, in
that month's issue. I want to write a letter,
but don't know the forwarding address.

Then, I thought I saw, a man, not like
me, he didn't push open doors, or go into
coffee shops, or buy a train ticket, and go, to
the station. Reaching the entrance, that man,
makes a strange motion, and then turns back.
That man is riding a bicycle. I'm usually very
quiet in crowds, but this time I couldn't keep
from talking to him. I thought, I started,
talking to, him. But my speech, didn't
bridge, that place. I tried to talk, but it
didn't become, conversation. The conversa-
tion, was floating in the sky, gazing at me.
And then I was, standing there, my mind
open, blank.

And, that, month's issue, didn't list, your,
name. I didn't know the forwarding address.
But, by that strange figure, I stole a glance
at some postcards, their addresses, and, my
spirit, started shaking loose. It was like that.

My dear.

I wonder how business-reply cards are
folded. Probably the shape of a postcard.
Even an old-style diary has a "letters mailed"
and a "letters received" column. Which one
comes first. That puzzles me. Hello, hello,
that phone is shaped like a question mark.
Holding, holding a palm a glance-over-the-
shoulder shape, I wondered what kind of
shape that could be. So I asked a mailman
that I met on a street corner. He stopped his
bicycle in the middle of the hill, and
remarked that there is a strange kind of U-

turn. It's a bad drawing, but please look at it:

At the top of the hill, the mailman says, he makes a U-turn. This time he'll go once around and then come down. A motorcycle wouldn't be handy, he said, because the hill is a one-way street. But it's okay with a bicycle. So even on rainy, or snowy, days, he delivers mail on a bicycle. Mounting the saddle, the mailman goes back the way he came. I was surprised to hear this U-turn story. (Is it funny?) But marathons have U-turns, too, don't they? And there's a road marker for the U-turns in a marathon. (Funny, this mailman said he runs 15 miles on his days off.) The way a letter is folded, the perforations on a business reply card, is it strange to think of? To be sure we'll get an answer, we sometimes put a blank page at the end of a letter. This is a mysterious U-turn. A ray of light becomes a shadow, sometimes, when you realize morning has already come. So I'm adding a clean sheet.

"May I have a reply?"

Glancing over his shoulder, but naturally, your, form, wasn't there. Turning a calendar page, looking for your name, but in that month's issue, you, you, you,

your name, wasn't, there. But, oddly, there, was, the entrance, there was, the exit, and the green light of the escape hatch, the belt-like light, expanding.

fold
/
listen to
/breath.

Planting an eggplant on open land, I want to end my life
        quietly _____, my spirit is in turmoil.

There's a high wind warning off Sanriku _____ fishermen
        please be careful.

      Tha/ that's /'s, it

Oh   Wind _____

      Ne.

The magic walk goes on. Sunset, my spirit and I go forth. Escape hatch, I start
wandering in the cosmos. Long since I lost my ticket, but within my body I still
feel a strange energy. Fluting and the escape hatch. I am moving through a crowd.
(I, a being between man   and woman.)   Sunset, my spirit and I go forth.

   . . .

[1]*ne* (neh): very common in Japanese conversation ("don't you agree?"; "you understand?!"), it
engages the listener, emphasizes what's been said, or left unsaid, can carry a range of emotional
coloring.

[2]Jōmon: The neolithic Jōmon period extended from about 8,000 to 200 B.C. A stone circle for solar
    worship dating from 4–5,000 B.C. was found at the foot of sacred Mt. Yatsugatake in
    central Honshu.

TRANSLATORS/TRANSLATIONS

AKAI TOSHIO:

TADA CHIMAKO, "Jungle Gym" (This version revised by the poet and TF)

BRENDA BARROWS:

YOSHIMASU GŌZŌ, from "Cradle: a Thousand Steps"

CHRISTOPHER DRAKE:

TAMURA RYŪICHI, all the poems

ŌOKA MAKOTO, Introduction: "Modern Japanese Poetry: Realities and Challenges"
                 Introduction: "*Renga*—Linked Poems"
                 Poems: "Water Region," "Soul Region," "Firefly Region"

MIURA MASASHI, Introduction: "Ōoka Makoto"
                 Introduction: "Tanikawa Shuntarō"

IIJIMA KŌICHI, Introduction: "Yoshimasu Gōzō"

WILLIAM I. ELLIOT AND KAMURA KAZUO:

TANIKAWA SHUNTARŌ, all the poems

CHRISTAN FLOOD AND KINOSHITA TETSUO:

SHIRAISHI KAZUKO, all the poems

KORIYAMA NAOSHI AND EDWARD LUEDERS:

TADA CHIMAKO, "Me," "Dead Sun," "Wind Invites Wind," "A Poetry Calendar," "Song," "The Odyssey or 'On Absence'" (These versions revised by the poet and TF)

TAKAKO LENTO:

ŌOKA MAKOTO, "For Spring," "Portrait," "When First You Saw Your Body," "The Power in a Starry Sky," "The Slope of That Hill," "A Woman I Often Dream Of," "For a Girl in Springtime" (These versions revised by the poet and TF)

ONUMA TADAYOSHI:

YOSHIOKA MINORU, all the poems

IIJIMA KŌICHI, all the poems

ŌOKA MAKOTO, "The Colonel and I," "Words/Words" (These versions revised by the poet and TF)

TSURUOKA YOSHIHISA, Introduction: "Yoshioka Minoru"
                 Introduction: "Iijima Kōichi"

KIRSTEN VIDAEUS:

TADA CHIMAKO, "King's Army," "Lost Kingdom," "Universe of the Rose" (These versions revised by the poet and TF)

鏡と鏡のたわむれ